FIFTY-TWO SIMPLE WAYS
TO MAKE A DIFFERENCE

PAUL SIMON

Augsburg Books

MINNEAPOLIS

To
Abner and Zoe Mikva
and
Tony and Leah Scariano,
friends for almost
fifty years
and great public servants

FIFTY-TWO SIMPLE WAYS TO MAKE A DIFFERENCE

Copyright © 2004 the Estate of Paul Simon. All rights reserved. Except for brief quotations in critical articles or reviews, no part of this book may be reproduced in any manner without prior written permission from the publisher. Write to: Permissions, Augsburg Fortress, Box 1209, Minneapolis, MN 55440.

Large-quantity purchases or custom editions of this book are available at a discount from the publisher. For more information, contact the sales department at Augsburg Fortress, Publishers, 1-800-328-4648, or write to: Sales Director, Augsburg Fortress, Publishers, P.O. Box 1209, Minneapolis, MN 55440-1209.

ISBN 0-8066-4678-0

Cover design by Dave Meyer
Cover photo by Steve Buhman, SIUC Media & Communication Resources
Book design by Michelle L. N. Cook

The paper used in this publication meets the minimum requirements of American National Standard for Information Sciences—Permanence of Paper for Printed Library Materials, ANSI Z329.48-1984. ♾ ™

Manufactured in the U.S.A.

08   07   06   05   04   1   2   3   4   5   6   7   8   9   10

ACKNOWLEDGMENTS

Ideas for this book came from many sources, as well as from my personal experiences, but I am particularly grateful to Chris Barr, Matthew Baughman, Gene Callahan, Helen Deniston, Robert Flannery, Woody and Terry Gump, John and Lois Hayward, John and Nancy Jackson, Mike and Marianne Lawrence, Zoe Mikva, Manjunath Pendakur, Arthur Simon, Julie and Martin Simon, Sheila Simon, and Perry Knop. Patti Simon read the manuscript and also tolerated my isolating myself in my study while working on it. Marilyn Lingle started to put my scribbling and typing into shape for a publisher, but back surgery halted that and then Pam Gwaltney took over and did most of the deciphering and getting the final product into a computer. I am grateful also to the people at Augsburg Fortress for their encouragement. Like in any book, I appreciate the help I received, but the errors of judgment are mine, not theirs.

CONTENTS

FOREWORD

BY JACK DANFORTH,
FORMER U.S. SENATOR, MISSOURI

THROUGHOUT HIS ILLUSTRIOUS PUBLIC LIFE, IN TOWN HALL meetings and call-in radio programs, at county fairs and Rotary luncheons, Paul Simon has heard a multitude of questions prefaced by the same seven words: "What are you going to do about . . . ?" The question might pertain to health care or the environment or education, but the first seven words are the same. It is as though the public official has the answer to every problem, and the responsibility of the citizen is exhausted by asking a question.

Not wanting to seem unresponsive to public demand, most people in public life offer ready solutions to the most complex problems, especially before elections. The gist of the response is, "I have a program that will make things better, elect me."

So it is not at all typical for a politician, present or past, to say as Paul Simon does in the preface of this book, "[C]hange is rarely achieved in a single, dramatic action. Change occurs because—little by little—people of good will, or those whose motives are not good, act."

Paul Simon never was a typical politician. Politics is a high energy occupation, but who else has the energy to author twenty-two books? Of course, the very fact that Paul felt compelled to write those books testifies to the premise behind this one: Public responsibility extends far beyond passing legislation.

Where watching "reality" shows on television seems preferable to doing real things, the desire to delegate civic responsibility to others is understandable. But it is not excusable. The fact is that anyone can help make the world better, so everyone should.

This is a "how-to" book—not how to play golf or how to build a cabinet, but how to be a good person. It is written from experience by someone who is just that. Much of its advice is practical and specific. (If you want to participate in an adult literacy program, Paul tells you just the organizations to contact). Some advice reminds us of what all of us know we should do, but sometimes ignore: Say thank you, tell people they are doing a good job.

While this is a how-to book, it contains some very big thoughts that deserve special emphasis.

One of these thoughts underlies the chapter, "Join a Church or Temple or Mosque." It is an important chapter, because the reason Paul gives for joining a religious congregation has nothing to do with an individualistic need to win for oneself personal salvation. Indeed, the question raised in the chapter is not, "What must I do to be saved?" but how can I join with others to do the saving work for our neighbors that God calls us to do. In Paul Simon's words, "People working together do charitable acts they would not perform in isolation." This emphasis on serving the community more than the self is at the heart of the book.

A second thought deserving special emphasis is Paul's view of the contributions ordinary citizens can make to their government.

Many people seem to think that the work of government is esoteric, requiring hidden knowledge available only to those on the inside. When I served in the Senate with Paul, many constituents approached me, usually in hushed tones, and asked if I would confide in them what was really going on in Washington. In fact, what most insiders do each morning is read *The Washington Post,* mining its pages for precisely the same information disclosed hours later in hearings held by senate committees. Anyone can learn all that is necessary to participate fully in our democracy. All one needs to do is take the time to be informed.

This is the point Paul makes in his chapter, "Don't Duck Your Civic Responsibilities." Good citizenship begins with keeping informed about public issues. For those who choose not to participate in government, ignorance is no excuse.

Nor is it an excuse to claim, as some do, that it does no good to talk to politicians, because politicians don't listen. The opposite is the case. If anything, politicians listen to a fault, utilizing opinion polling and focus groups to test public opinion. They care about what you think, because that determines their ability to keep their jobs. As Paul observes, there is no doubt that involved citizens influence public policy. Good government is not something we should leave to the experts. Good government is the responsibility of each of us.

Paul Simon's premise is that ordinary people doing small things can make a big difference. The irony is that this manifestly correct observation comes from an extraordinary person who has done big things.

PREFACE

ONE OF THE DISCOURAGEMENTS OF PUBLIC LIFE DAY AFTER day is to see people who have the potential to contribute so much to building a better society—and they don't do it. They may decline to participate because they do not understand that change is rarely achieved in a single, dramatic action. Change occurs because—little by little—people of good will, or those whose motives are not good, act.

Between those two extremes is a huge body of humanity that is either indifferent or who view themselves as helpless. Those who are indifferent are not likely to read this book. It is addressed primarily to people of good will who are either comfortable in their irresponsibility, or who have no idea how much positive change they can achieve with a little effort. Occasionally I see a bumper sticker: "Do Some Random Act of Kindness Today!" That "random act" results not only in helping society, but in helping the one who acts.

The examples I use are frequently from Illinois because that's where I live. If you look around wherever you are, you will find counterparts to these people. Fifty-two is not a magic number, but if each week you examine one of these suggestions, in one year you will be a changed person, and you will have helped to improve our world. You may want to start with following through on one a month. Or it may be that only a few ideas in the book strike you as things you want to do. Whatever you do will bene-fit you and others. After reading the book, you might want your religious or civic organization to use part of their time each week to discuss one chapter.

You will not find a pattern in the book, in part because the fingers of each idea almost always encompass more than one area, and in part so that you will read through the book and not skip to an area already familiar to you. Reading about the unfamiliar may be more meaningful than reading within your comfort zone.

Let me make one immediate suggestion: If this is your book—not one from the library or loaned to you by a friend— get out a pen or marker and highlight the things you would like to consider doing.

The ideas in this book have come from several people. No one can do all of these things well; certainly I don't. But we can be motivated to do better—and that makes a huge difference.

—Paul Simon

1

INVITE A COUPLE OR FAMILY
OF ANOTHER RACE OR RELIGION
OR ETHNIC GROUP TO YOUR HOME
FOR DINNER

WE NEED TO LEARN THE BASIC LESSON THAT HUMANITY IS NOT divisible. If you have acquired a PhD or MD and haven't learned this truth, you are poorly educated. In this country and around the world, we need to reach out to each other, to learn our hopes and our problems, our dreams and our difficulties. Sitting around a table visiting with people of differing backgrounds is a good starting point. It takes a little courage to extend that first invitation, but you won't regret doing it. And don't worry if your furniture has a used look and the tablecloth is soiled, the key is the warmth of your welcome, not the superficial things.

The habit of inviting guests for a meal is, unfortunately, a declining part of our culture. Even getting our own families together for dinner is less common. Both customs are worth reviving.

To help "break the ice," invite one or two members of the other family to join you for lunch or coffee to become more acquainted. Sometimes this makes the dinner invitation to your home a little easier for both you and your guests. If you have young children in your family, talk with them about the background and culture of the people who will be visiting you.

Another way to ease any discomfort you might have in hosting a couple or family is to invite other couples or families to join you.

As I was typing this manuscript (yes, on a manual typewriter!), a woman called on another matter and I told her the reason she caught me at home is that I am working on this book. She asked about the topic, and when I told her, she mentioned that they had a guest from Pakistan visit them. "He opened my eyes," she related. "I had never known anyone of the Islamic faith. We had a great and candid discussion."

It would not take a huge effort for you to repeat that experience ten times and for a wider circle to do it hundreds or even thousands of times. What a difference that could make in the relationships between the United States and other nations.

One thing I like to do when we have guests—and have the time to do it—is go around the table during dessert and ask one question of each guest. After the question is asked and answered, everyone can discuss it. This helps your quiet but thoughtful guests join more fully in the discussion. For your guests of differing backgrounds, consider what questions you can ask that will evoke discussion but not embarrass them.

My family's dining room table seats eight or ten people comfortably, which is ideal for good discussion. Occasionally we'll host more than that, and then we serve food buffet style. With scattered seating, you'll have to work harder to instigate a discussion that gets everyone involved, including your guests of differing backgrounds.

This type of hospitality will enrich your life, lead to stimulating evenings, and move us ahead on the road to better understanding.

INVITE TWO INTERNATIONAL STUDENTS TO YOUR HOME FOR DINNER

I SUGGEST INVITING TWO STUDENTS BECAUSE IF ONE IS SHY, your dialogue may be more difficult. But one is still better than none. Most colleges or universities have international students. If you live near a school, extend the invitation. Someone at the school would be pleased to receive your inquiry and can tell you how to proceed. Civic organizations such as the Rotary Club and a number of religious groups sponsor exchanges for high school students, which is another opportunity to learn from each other.

Recently, I spoke to a group of international students at a university and I asked how many of them had been in a U.S. home for a visit. Only two students raised their hands. That indicates a missed opportunity for many international students to understand our country better, and a missed chance for American families to understand another part of the world better. Embarrassment of our lack of knowledge about another country is sometimes a barrier to such an invitation. Reading about your guests' home countries can be worthwhile, but it is not essential. Ask questions and you will find the students eager to talk about their homeland. Most are proud of their nation, just as we are proud of ours, and they welcome finding Americans who want to learn more about their country. This is important, because many of the international students studying in the United States today will be leaders in their countries tomorrow. You can help create an atmosphere of friendship and understanding between our nations.

Approximately 580,000 international students are in our colleges and universities. We should get to know them better, and they should get to know us better. The foreign students who study in the United States are more reflective of the world's population spread than are the students who study in other nations. Only slightly more than one percent of U.S. college students study abroad for a summer or semester, and two-thirds of them study in western Europe. Ninety-five percent of the world's population growth in the next fifty years will occur in the developing nations, the countries U.S. students studying abroad too often avoid.

One reason international students attend school here is because they want to get to know us and our culture better. We should give them more opportunities for that. We are 4 percent of the world's population. If we want a stable and peaceful future for our children and generations to come, we will have to pay more attention to the other 96 percent of the earth's people.

The tragedy of September 11th happened in part because of our insensitivity to the people and problems of other countries. That insensitivity often comes across to people of other nations as arrogance. With a simple invitation to your home, you can do something to help change that image.

HELP SOMEONE SUFFERING FROM "THE WORST DISEASE"

A WOMAN I KNEW SLIGHTLY CAME INTO MY OFFICE AND, acknowledging my help for fundraising drives for everything from cancer to Alzheimer's, she said she was suffering from the worst disease in the world. Startled, I asked her what it was. She responded, "I'm not wanted." I remember being stunned by her reply. She and her son lived in a small town where ordinarily people greet each other and think they know each other. But not many really knew her. I doubt that her neighbors understood her.

Find a person in your neighborhood or in an organization to which you belong who appears a little shy or lonely. Go out of your way to be friendly, perhaps by sharing tomatoes from your garden or homemade brownies, or by including this person in a lunch you have with friends. Greet this person warmly by name.

In the song, "Mr. Cellophane," from the award-winning movie and play, *Chicago,* one of the characters describes the way people regard him. He feels so transparent and of so little substance to others that he says people can see right past him and never really know he is in the same room as they are.[1]

There are too many Mr. and Mrs. Cellophanes—people we see but don't really see. It doesn't take a lot of effort to extend yourself just a little. For instance, when you get on an elevator you can say, "good morning" or some other appropriate greeting.

Being friendly to the person in the line with you at the grocery store might seem like a simple thing, but to the other person, it might mean a lot more. I once gave a young disabled man a ride home on a rainy day from the grocery store, only six blocks away. It happened over three years ago, but whenever I see the young man, he mentions it. It had more meaning to him than simply getting out of the rain; someone was paying attention to him. Someone cared.

Here are two things you can do:

First, learn the first and last names of your immediate neighbors and go out of your way to greet them by name the next time you see them.

Second, for one week, at least three times a day say hello and make conversation with a person you might not ordinarily greet. Ask someone on crutches what happened, compliment someone for having a great smile, tell the clerk in that grocery store that you really appreciate his or her good service, or find something friendly to say to a stranger or an acquaintance. Use your imagination, and then apply it three times a day for one week.

I doubt that you'll stop after one week.

And fewer people will say to themselves, "I'm not wanted."

4

SCHEDULE TWO TELEVISION-FREE
DAYS AND NIGHTS

EACH WEEK, TAKE A BREAK FROM WATCHING TELEVISION (WITH the possible exception of the news) for two days and nights. Include computer and video games in the prohibition, except for studies that require the use of the computer. Plan activities on those two evenings that will enrich your family life: attend a PTA meeting, read a book, or do something to help yourself or others.

Social researcher Robert Putnam notes: "Time diaries show that husbands and wives spend three or four times as much time watching television together as they spend talking to each other, and six to seven times as much as they spend in community activities outside the home. Moreover, as the number of TV sets per household multiplies, even watching together becomes rarer."[2]

Think about this important observation of mine (but I don't have any research for it): Leaders in almost any field watch little television.

Children can be hurt by television. Entertainment television violence causes harm, as solid research shows. The American Medical Association, the American Academy of Pediatrics, the National Institute of Mental Health, the Centers for Disease Control, and many others warn us about entertainment television and video games that glorify violence—as a lot of them do. Nielsen studies found that children in the United States ages two to eleven watch an average of three hours and sixteen minutes of television a day. Research by a commission established by the National Association of State Universities and Land-Grant Colleges to determine why students don't write well, found that "most fourth-graders spend less than three hours a week writing, which is about 15 percent of the time they spend watching television."[3] The American Medical Association reported that children "who watch more than ten hours of TV each week are more likely to be overweight, aggressive, and slow to learn in school."[4] A University of Michigan survey for the American Psychological Association concluded: "Both males and females from all social strata and all levels of initial aggressiveness are placed at increased risk for the development of adult aggressive and violent behavior when they view a high and steady diet of violent TV shows in early childhood."[5] John P. Murray of Kansas State University, whose research on children's brains is supported by the University of Texas, Harvard, and others, told a congressional committee: "Viewing entertainment video violence . . . is treated by the [child's] brain as a real event that is threatening and worthy of being stored for long-term memory in an area of the brain that makes recall of the events almost instantaneous. . . . We see normal children storing away violent images in a manner that could be used to guide future behavior."[6]

Television commercials also appeal to the greed that is a part of each of us. Buy this car and you'll find happiness. This rug will make your home beautiful. That toy is something all children need to have. This soap will make your skin beautiful, and that toothpaste will make your teeth whiter, so you can attract a marvelous boyfriend or girlfriend. And on and on and on. These advertisements are part of a free society, but everything that is permitted is not necessarily good. We are urged to use our financial resources to acquire products, a highly imbalanced view of life. We rarely see the problems of the poor in our nation or in other nations. No mention is made of the environmental harm from overconsumption. The message from television commercials—and too many TV shows—is that buying what they are selling is the key to a better life. The individual ads may not be falsified, but the sum total of the messages is a kind of false advertising that says satisfaction in life comes from acquiring things. The reality is that satisfaction in life comes from sharing.

Veteran actor Hal Holbrook once commented in an interview, "This machine [pointing to a television set] has been the most powerful instrument of destruction I've seen in my lifetime."[7]

Two nights away from television will be good for your family and for our world.

5

"You Get What You Give"

ONCE, WHEN I WAS SPEAKING AT A CONFERENCE ON MENTAL health and our prisons, sponsored by Capital University and the Ohio Supreme Court, I stayed at the Radisson Airport Hotel in Columbus, Ohio. I arrived late at night, and the next morning I went into the small gift shop to buy newspapers. An unusually pleasant man greeted me. I assumed from his appearance that the gentleman was retired and working part-time in the shop. Later that afternoon, I stopped in again to get something to drink, and I told him that his warm greeting earlier that morning improved my day.

"You meet wonderful people here from all over the world," he responded with enthusiasm. I mentioned that we generally create a pleasant or unpleasant atmosphere, based more on our own attitude than by what others do and say. He agreed and added, "You get what you give." I had never heard it phrased so simply and accurately.

His name is Wayne Wilson. He retired from the Air Force after twenty-one years of service. He leases the gift shop from the hotel and has been in that small business for two decades. "I just took advantage of the opportunities that came my way," he says. Wayne Wilson provides customers with much more than newspapers, toothpaste, and the usual gift shop sundries. He makes people walk out of his small shop feeling better. Just as hatred and bitterness are contagious, so are friendliness and warmth.

I've traveled to more than one hundred countries. Periodically someone will tell me, "People are not friendly there." I have yet to find a place where most people are not friendly. Be good and friendly to others, and they will respond to you in the same way. On rare occasions you may encounter people with a "chip on their shoulder" who do not respond to a warm greeting. They exist in every country, but those people have personal problems, and they are not typical of citizens anywhere.

"You get what you give," Wayne Wilson says.

He is correct.

Be a giver.

6

REGISTER TO BECOME
AN ORGAN DONOR

I TRIED TO HELP SAVE THE LIFE OF AN ELEVEN-YEAR-OLD GIRL named Melannie Veliz from Aurora, Illinois. She was a bright-eyed straight-A student, who wanted to become a librarian. But Melannie faced many obstacles in her young life. For starters, she had cystic fibrosis and needed a lung transplant. Her parents were from Chile. They came to the United States believing that somehow in this generous country they could find help for Melannie. Their legal status complicated things, but with assistance from Senator Dick Durbin and Congressman Luis Gutierrez they were able to work around that problem. The cost for a lung transplant was $450,000, but thanks to many generous contributors— including Melannie's classmates—the money was raised for the transplant. Finally, after too many months, Melannie was put on the waiting list for a transplant.

Unfortunately, there is a severe shortage of organ donors. Not enough people sign cards and letters saying that when they die, their organs can be used to save someone else's life. So Melannie had to wait, gradually declining in health, and died. It was a race between the awful disease and the availability of a child's lung. The legal and financial complications that delayed getting her on the list may have killed her, but the lack of lungs available for transplant almost certainly did. St. Louis Children's Hospital, one of the two hospitals in this country that performs this operation on children, told me that fifty-eight children have died while on the waiting list. Ideally, an ailing young person would receive a child's lung, but sometimes a partial lung from an adult can be used instead. If more people become organ donors, by simply signing the forms that give permission for their organs to be used after their death to save another life, the chances of survival for others like Melannie, will greatly improve.

Sign up now to be an organ donor. Tell your family your wishes and check with a hospital or law office about a form to create "a living will"—a statement that you want your body parts to save others' lives—or make out a "power of attorney" statement, authorizing someone to act for you in the event of your death or disability, with clear instructions to that person to have your body used to give life to others after your death. Many states also have a simple form that certifies you as an organ donor, which you can sign when you get your driver's license.

If you don't make organ donor arrangements now, your family may be reluctant to make this decision during a time of great grief. I know. My father died of leukemia, and I am certain he would have wanted his organs to save other lives. But when my father only had hours to live and the hospital staff asked us, my mother could not stand the thought of taking parts from his body. Should I have pushed her more on this? Probably, but it is difficult to push this issue when in the throes of serious emotional hurdles. We should have taken that step when my father was in good health and able to voice his own opinion. I have given organ donor instructions to my family. To give someone the chance to live after you die is a great gift. If more people had done that, Melannie Veliz might be alive today, dreaming about becoming a librarian.

Make a note for yourself to become an organ donor before the end of this month.

A creative person at the University of Wisconsin developed T-shirts with this message: "Don't take your organs to heaven. Heaven knows we need them here."

Related to this issue is another important contribution you can make: Donate blood to the Red Cross. You might not like to get stuck by a needle. No one does. But that pain is minor and only lasts for seconds, while the benefits—which you are unlikely to see—could mean a prolonged and healthier life for someone in need. Even better, volunteer to assist in your community when the Red Cross comes around. After September 11th, people overwhelmed the local blood donor drives for a few weeks, and then the interest diminished. But the need still exists.

7

Join a Church or Temple
or Mosque

GOOD INTENTIONS OF DOING SOMETHING CONSTRUCTIVE FOR society are much more effective—and more likely to take place—when part of a group endeavor. You can help guide the group into an avenue of service. In his book *Bowling Alone,* Robert Putnam notes that "religious adherents are more likely to contribute time and money to activities beyond their own congregation."[8] One survey concluded: "Young people who say that they attend religious services weekly are much more civically and politically engaged than other youth, especially those who say that they never attend services. They volunteer much more regularly, they are much more confident in their own capacity to 'make a difference,' they trust other people more, they vote more and consider voting important, and they are much more likely to hold positive views of government. This engagement holds true even if income, race, and education are controlled."[9] People who profess religious inclinations but don't belong to any religious organization are less likely to act on those inclinations in concrete ways. Associating with others in those endeavors stimulates us, helps us. A religious organization—church, temple, or mosque—gives people an avenue to help others in a structured and meaningful way. People working together do charitable acts they would not perform in isolation, and working with a group in an activity that has a positive outcome is enjoyable.

The religious community has had an impact on everything from world hunger to civil rights to meals for the homeless; from assistance to people in earthquakes and floods to getting food and education to the world's impoverished. If someone comes to me with a serious problem that has somehow "fallen through the cracks" of help provided through traditional social service agencies, I frequently call a member of the clergy, regardless if the person in need has a religious affiliation. Religious groups usually can provide a positive.

For example, the Roman Catholic Church of the Holy Spirit in Carterville, Illinois, assigns a "grandparent" to a child twice a year, so that all of their children can experience the pleasure of friendship with an older person. This friendship is mutually beneficial, boosting the morale of the senior citizen as well.

Religion, as it is practiced and not merely professed, also can be a powerful force for harm. Even in the United States we have a history of "down moments" in the practice of religion, times when anti-Semitism or anti-Catholicism and, more recently, anti-Muslim passions twist religion from a positive factor of help to one of harm.

Charles Kimball, a Baptist minister and author of the book *When Religion Becomes Evil*, noted: "The most powerful and pervasive force in human society, bringing out the best and worst in people [is religion]. . . . More wars have been waged, more people killed, and more evil perpetrated in the name of religion than by any other institutional force. . . . A good dose of humility is important for all of us when we talk about truth from God."[10] Kimball continues: "Corruption of religion in the context of protecting or defending something considered sacred is all too common."[11]

A 2002 survey of Americans regarding the interaction between people of differing faiths is not encouraging. The survey found that only 51 percent of Americans know someone who is

Jewish, only 28 percent know a Muslim, and an even smaller 17 percent know a Hindu or Buddhist. In this day, it is particularly significant that nearly three-fourths of all Americans do not personally know a member of the Muslim faith, the world's second largest religion.

A number of books are available to help you better understand the beliefs and faith practices of others. Among them is the popular For Dummies series and the Idiot Guides series.[12] Both contain books on many of the world's religions. They provide at least a minimal guide to understanding these faiths. I occasionally hear, "But I don't find myself in complete agreement with any religious group." Of course not. Few people agree 100 percent with the views of any religious group. People who agree 100 percent with any faith's doctrinal views aren't thinking. And that small minority of zealots are the ones most likely to cause harm.

While I have not experienced as many attacks from religious extremists as some office-holders and theologians, occasionally I do get a venom-filled letter from someone who is sincere but distorted, who sees the errors of others but does not recognize his or her own flaws. Such people often believe that their interpretation of a religious faith is superior to all others. Unfortunately, righteous indignation is too often unrighteous indignation. Rigidity in religion is no more beneficial than it is in any other field.

But let me be clear about this: That some people twist religious beliefs, sometimes into hatred that can lead to violence, is not a reason to avoid religious affiliation. We should take our religious beliefs seriously, while respecting those of others. We should be walking the path toward interfaith tolerance.

None of us is perfect, and the religious groups with which we may affiliate are not perfect. But that should not be a barrier to becoming a member of a faith-based organization or living out our faith in the acts of love and service.

8

Join a Nonreligious Organization That Has the Potential to Do Constructive Things

THE LIST OF POSSIBILITIES IS LONG: THE ROTARY CLUB, THE National Association for the Advancement of Colored People (NAACP), Business and Professional Women, the Mental Health Association, or a senior citizen's group, to name a few. Joining a large group of people can be a great opportunity for you to stretch your creativity and your get-things-done muscles. It can also expand your list of contacts. The more people you are acquainted with and the more you broaden your base of knowledge, the more likely you are to know who to call for information or assistance on a project. This helps improve the likelihood of getting things accomplished. Affiliating with a larger group can benefit the larger society.

Having more contacts may ultimately help you financially, but I am not recommending participation because it will help you financially. You can expand your vision and service beyond that narrow financial base. For example, by joining a Special Olympics Committee, which sponsors athletic events for people with disabilities, it is unlikely you'll benefit one penny. But the rewards you will receive go beyond any monetary satisfaction.

Jot down the names of six organizations in your area that do good things to help the public at large or a sector of the public. Next, contact a friend who is a member of an organization that appeals to you and tell him or her that you want to participate.

You will be enriched.

9

REMEMBER ROBERT REID

YOU MAY HAVE NEVER HEARD OF HIM, BUT YOU SHOULD NOT ever forget him. Sixty seven-year-old Robert Reid has a physical disability, and when he speaks you immediately notice a speech impediment. Born in Chicago, he came to rural southern Illinois and worked at the Little Grassy outdoor camp and recreational facility near Southern Illinois University for nineteen years. Gradually his cerebral palsy problems worsened, and he could no longer continue his work. He realized that leaving Little Grassy caused a void in his life. "I was very lonely," he recalls. "I wanted to be close to the students."

But Robert Reid, who many people would describe as not able to do much, on August 26, 1993 (he recalls the date precisely), started what has become a part of the culture of the university. Every morning, he gets on his bicycle and makes the rounds of the flagpoles on campus at Carbondale and raises the flags. Later in the day he takes them down. When the clock in the campus tower stops or gains or loses time, he lets the university leaders know about it immediately. Robert Reid contributes more to this campus than most—and receives no pay.

Phil Hartzell and Willard Ice are two more people with whom you are likely not familiar. Both are no longer living. When I served in the state legislature, Phil wrote letters and more letters. He always knew what he was talking about, and he was able to influence the course of legislation. Willard Ice, a lawyer, had an unusual grasp of the revenue situation Illinois faced and told legislators the minutest bits of information. He later became director of the Department of Revenue for Illinois. What I haven't told you is that Phil was severely disabled with multiple sclerosis and Willard was blind.

Joe Hartzler and Roger Irving are two more people worth remembering. You may not recall the name Joe Hartzler, but a few years ago you saw and heard it. He served as chief prosecutor for the federal government in the case against Timothy McVeigh, the bomber of the Oklahoma City Federal Building. Reporters praised the thorough job Joe Hartzler and his staff did. What rarely received any attention is that Joe Hartzler has multiple sclerosis and is confined to a wheelchair.

Roger Irving became a person of major influence and a widely respected leader in the Illinois state government, serving as assistant director of three different departments. While serving in the military, he suffered an accident that caused him to become a quadriplegic. His mobility was confined to movement in a wheelchair. But he went on to graduate from Illinois College and earned his master's degree from UCLA. What might have stopped most people from public service did not stop Roger Irving, and we are all beneficiaries of his work.

Robert Reid, Phil Hartzell, Willard Ice, Joe Hartzler, and Roger Irving should inspire all of us. Did they have disabilities? Yes. Do all of us have some type of handicap? Yes. But the biggest barrier most of us have is indifference.

There are unsung heroes in your community, people who so easily could have used a barrier as an excuse for coasting through the rest of their lives, but they have not done that.

Maybe there is one more unsung hero where you live. You.

10

FIND AN ISSUE ABOUT WHICH
YOU FEEL STRONGLY

IT MAY BE MENTAL HEALTH OR RACE RELATIONS OR THE adequacy of your local school system. When you feel strongly about a certain issue, you can grumble to your friends, complain to your coworkers, sulk—or you can do something about it.

Invite six creative friends to your home for an evening to talk about the subject you select and what you might do about it. Then follow through. Invite other friends who may share in this concern for an informal evening work session. Keep the food for the evening simple. Ideally this meeting should take place in the privacy of a home rather than a noisy restaurant. An office will do if those invited are too geographically scattered, though an office tends to be a little "cold" in its atmosphere. People should feel comfortable and free to contribute their ideas. Provide paper, so ideas can be recorded as they emerge. By the end of the evening, you'll probably have at least twenty questionable ideas, but you also should have two or three solid possibilities. Build on one or two of them.

A key to being effective is creativity. A "bull session" like the one described usually will result in creative ideas. There are two advantages to this type of small gathering to brainstorm: First, you will each stretch each other, developing good ideas no one had considered before the meeting; and second, your service idea will attract other adherents as a result of the meeting. Your quest for service will seem like a less lonely project.

11

BECOME A HUMAN OUTDOOR
CLEAN-UP MACHINE

APPROXIMATELY FORTY YEARS AGO, I WALKED TO A MEETING
with Irving Dilliard, the prize-winning editor of the editorial
page of the *St. Louis Post-Dispatch*. As we strolled, he occasionally
stopped to pick up a beer can or a candy wrapper. He explained
it was a little way to improve the world and it gave him extra
exercise each day, exercise that might enable him to live longer.
(He lived to be ninety-six!)

I am not as faithful about picking up things as Irving Dilliard,
but I do it. A few weeks ago near Edwardsville, Illinois, I saw a
man doing the same thing. I stopped and asked him why. He said
that a St. Louis journalist, whose name he could not recall, did it,
and he was following that example. I told him the name of the
journalist. If each of us does this, even occasionally, others will
follow our example. If fifty people reading this book do this,
there will be at least two more following their good example. We
can make our communities and parks and campuses more attrac-
tive—and we will be healthier.

Millard Fuller, founder of Habitat for Humanity, relates his
experience and observation:

> Our house in Americus was located on East Church Street.
> My law office was about three quarters of a mile away on West

Church Street. As I walked to work each morning and back home in the evening, I got into the habit of picking up trash along the way. There was no fanfare to what I did. . . .

Also, my daily encounters with trash gave me an insight I had not had before: There is a direct connection between trash on the streets and substandard housing. A community that tolerates trash on the streets will accept substandard housing. Conversely, a community that will not accept trash will not tolerate poverty housing. You see, trash is a visible sign of the mentality of people in an area. That mentality is that the physical environment is of little concern to them. Substandard housing is simply a larger visible sign of a lack of concern.[13]

My daughter and son-in-law and their two daughters took a vacation to the west, and in two of the national parks they visited, the National Park personnel said they would make Junior Park Rangers of young people who picked up trash and turned it in. At one of the parks they provided a plastic bag, and at the other they did not. But my eight-year-old granddaughter, Brennan, took the task seriously and after handing in the trash she collected, she received a Junior Park Ranger Badge when they exited the park. Since then, my granddaughters have become much more sensitive about trash—particularly about smokers who leave their cigarette butts everywhere.

I can't give you a badge, but if you help pick up trash left behind, you can be proud knowing that you have helped the appearance of areas where your feet have trod, and that others will follow your example.

BE AN EARTH-SAVER

THERE ARE HUNDREDS OF SMALL THINGS WE CAN DO TO BE earth-savers: Riding a bicycle to work, choosing a particular light bulb, using recycled paper, saving gas by sharing rides to work, using solar energy. Or something as simple as where we put the hot water heater when we build a home, how we dispose of garbage, or creating a compost pile.

Earth-saving might even include encouraging restaurant owners to serve smaller portions. When we waste food, we also waste energy—and add to our obesity problems. Note these words from a leader on the world's food problems: "The amount Americans spend overeating and then dieting to deal with the consequences would be more than enough to wipe out world hunger."[14] European restaurants generally serve smaller portions.

My family built a passive solar home in southern Illinois in 1981. I was tempted to make it active solar, but I am not a "handyman." I didn't want to worry about broken pipes and panels. By building our home (designed by an environmentally sensitive architect) so that it faced south, we save energy, and we save money. Southern Illinois has below-zero temperatures only about one winter in five. But even on those days, if the sun is out, our furnace doesn't kick in until after the sun sets. My daughter and son-in-law hang their laundry outside to dry on sunny days. Dryers use nine times the electricity of washing machines. The list of possibilities is endless. And with almost every environmentally sensitive thing we do, we also save money.

One of many books filled with practical suggestions for helping the environment and saving money is *You Can Prevent Global Warming* by Jeffrey Langholz and Kelly Turner (Andrews McMeel Publishing, 2003). You'll find many ideas there.

There are small things that you may be able to do, depending on where you live:

Walk or bike to work instead of driving. Today in the United States, we have more cars and trucks than drivers.

If you farm and use irrigation, try drip irrigation if you can afford it. If not, put down a plastic sheet where the water flows until it reaches the point of land you want to irrigate.

Turn off the hot water heater in your home if you will be gone more than three days. It will save you money and help protect the earth from excessive energy consumption. There are new water heaters that work only on demand and save energy and money.

If you build a new home, consider making it passive solar and use heavy insulation. It pays off in dollars and results in a healthier world. Most existing houses can be made more efficient by adding insulation to the attic and walls, through caulking and weather-stripping, and by improving weather protection in the windows.

Write a letter to your legislators urging the creation of bike paths.

Talk to the person who picks up your garbage. Tell him or her that you would like to recycle newspapers, plastic bottles, and aluminum cans. Can your garbage collector help? If not, send a letter to the editor of the local newspaper suggesting that your community become more involved in recycling. It is likely to get a response. We are far behind Japan and many nations when it comes to recycling.

If you do not have recycling in your community, and your garbage collector cannot help, contact your mayor or city council member or other local officials and bring up the issue. Many communities have curbside recycling and a few states mandate it.

Let your legislators know that you would support an increase in the gas tax. I have four friends who drive hybrid gas-electric cars that are self-charging, ride comfortably and smoothly, and get forty-four to fifty miles per gallon, reducing air pollution greatly. The cost of the car: $20,500. An increase in the gas tax would encourage more Americans to buy fuel-efficient cars. Every penny increase results in purer air. A portion of the gas tax should go toward more research into alternative fuels, including a barely visible, still primitive source: solar energy.

Find an issue involving the earth's natural resources that interests you. Read about it. Learn what effects the abuse of nature has caused, or may cause. One issue that is going to become increasingly important is the earth's water supply. People who study this issue, even for just a few hours, come to realize we're heading toward a catastrophe. The United Nations reports that every day fourteen thousand people die because of poor water quality—ninety-five hundred of those are children. The situation will become much worse if we don't start planning to avoid this disaster. Become a well-informed and action-oriented citizen.

13

FOLLOW THE EXAMPLE OF BILL
AND GEORGIA CARSON

I KNEW BILL CARSON LONG BEFORE HIS RETIREMENT. HE AND his wife, Georgia, lived in Illinois and retired to Santa Fe, New Mexico. Shortly after they moved, they learned from school principal Vickie Sewing that the local Salazar Elementary School had a 37 percent turnover in students during the school year because of family movement and terrible test scores. Ninety percent of the students come from families with income below the federal poverty line. Bill and Georgia volunteered to help and recruited fellow members of the United Church. They now have seventy-eight volunteers, two-thirds from the church, who come to the school to read and listen to the students. All the volunteers are over fifty and most are retired or semi-retired. They include a former newspaper editor, a former CIA agent, a retired veterinarian, and a former Peace Corps worker. The Carsons made it clear to the teachers that the volunteers were there to help, not to run things. "It's important for teachers to know I'm available but not hovering," says Georgia. "I emphasize [that] with the volunteers. You're not here to make decisions."[15]

Salazar's test scores for its more than five hundred students have turned around. New Mexico's State Department of Education removed Salazar Elementary School from the list of those needing substantial improvement and changed its status to "a profile in excellence." The volunteers have formed a nonprofit corporation, Salazar Partnership, so they can receive contributions. Every year they give each student three new books. Now the program is beginning at another Santa Fe school. Bill and Georgia Carson have made their retirement years a helpful experience for young people in need—and enriching for themselves and other volunteers.

Obviously you do not have to be retired to make a contribution. And if you wait until your retirement years to perform public service, you are not likely to do it when retired. I am pleased at what Bill and Georgia are doing—but not surprised. It is part of the pattern of their life.

"Some day I will take more of an interest in political and civic life," people frequently tell me. But if people don't pay attention to the problems and potential of their community or to our nation or our world now, their time of service isn't likely to come. Retirement years do present special opportunities, but I have never heard anyone say, "I'm looking forward to retirement—I'm going to learn how to play golf and tennis." If you haven't learned the basics of these activities before retirement, it's unlikely you will suddenly develop an interest and skill. The same is true of service to people in need or contributing to political and civic life or working through your church or synagogue or mosque.

"How do you like retirement?" I asked a friend of many years.

"I'm bored," he responded. "I don't have anything to do." The truth is he prepared his bank account for retirement but not his life. He did not follow the path of Bill and Georgia Carson.

14

VOLUNTEER TO HELP AN ADULT
LEARN TO READ AND WRITE

IMAGINE NOT BEING ABLE TO READ BOOKS TO YOUR CHILDREN, not being able to read a street sign, or not being able to read the instructions on a prescription. The stories of people who once were illiterate and now are able to read are tearjerkers; the phrase I hear again and again is that it's like "being in prison." You might not be aware of it, but there are people where you live who are unable to read. They hide it, often from their own families, because they are ashamed.

When I served in the U.S. House of Representatives, I had "open office hours" in small communities in my district. Often I'd have to ask people to sign a consent form so I could get permission to access their records and files. Frequently someone would ask, "Is it okay if my wife [husband] signs?" I realized many people could not even sign their own names. Sometimes people said they forgot their reading glasses. Occasionally, someone would carefully and painfully draw his or her name; this person probably could write nothing else.

These experiences led me to work with then Secretary of Education Ted Bell and Barbara Bush, wife of the then vice president, as well as others on this immense problem. Eventually I sponsored the National Literacy Act, signed into law by the senior George Bush. It's helped move the nation ahead a little, though we still have a long way to go. Approximately three million adult

Americans cannot recognize their name in block print, and by the most conservative estimate, twenty-three million adult Americans cannot read a newspaper or fill out an employment form, a huge obstacle for their lives and our nation's productive capacity.

I am frequently asked, "What can we do to improve our schools?" There isn't just one answer to that question: children need more days in school (Illinois has 176 days of school per year, Germany 240, Japan 243, Singapore 280); schools need to teach foreign languages, a subject in which we are far behind other nations; communities need to spend at least as much money in poor neighborhoods as they do in wealthy neighborhoods; and so on. One thing that often gets overlooked: The need to improve the education of parents, who often lack basic skills. This educational opportunity will increase their income and self-confidence—but more importantly, it will help them help their children with schoolwork. Children who aren't exposed to books or newspapers or magazines at home, or whose parents are either illiterate or semi-literate, are at a huge disadvantage. A massive, well-publicized campaign is needed to recruit the volunteers that are necessary to help solve this problem.

It's not always easy to work with someone who has little or no literacy skills, but those volunteers who persevere will earn huge satisfaction from helping to create an immense positive change for someone. Contact your local library or area community college to find out if there are any volunteer opportunities. You may discover that no organization in your community has established an adult literacy program. This is common, but it presents you with a greater challenge and opportunity. Contact a national literacy organization that can assist you in launching a program in your area:

The Barbara Bush Foundation for Family Literacy
1201 15th Street NW, Suite 420
Washington, DC 20005
(202) 955-6183
www.barbarabushfoundation.com

National Center for Family Literacy
325 West Main Street, Suite 300
Louisville, KY 40202-4237
1-877-FAMLIT-1 (1-877-326-5481)
www.famlit.org

National Institute for Literacy
1775 I Street NW, Suite 730
Washington, DC 20006-2401
(202) 233-2025
novel.nifl.gov

ProLiteracy Worldwide
(merger of Laubach Literacy International
and Literacy Volunteers of America)
1320 Jamesville Avenue
Syracuse, NY 13210
1-888-528-2224
www.proliteracy.org

Reading Is Fundamental, Inc.
1825 Connecticut Avenue NW, Suite 400
Washington, DC 20009
1-877-RIF-READ (1-877-743-7323)
www.rif.org

It may take extra effort to start a program from scratch—but imagine how difficult it is for someone who cannot read or write to find help. If you do volunteer in adult literacy and have a good experience, write a letter to the local newspaper and share what the experience meant to your student (who may be sixty-five years old) and to you. This can multiply your good work by encouraging others to join the literacy crusade.

15

Do Something Not Associated with Your Day-to-Day Work

SOMETIMES THE LEAST LIKELY ACTIVITIES CAN SPARK SOMETHING inside of you. One advantage to doing something not associated with your ordinary daily routine is that it can turn on your creative juices and help bring a fresh approach to your work. It brings you into contact with new people and opens up a whole new world. For example, Bono, the lead singer of the Irish rock band U2, somehow persuaded U.S. Secretary of Treasury Paul O'Neill to accompany him on a trip to Africa. O'Neill came back a changed man.

But your activity doesn't have to be as drastic as flying all the way to Africa. During college, I had little interest in science, but Dana College in Blair, Nebraska, the excellent small liberal arts school I attended for two years, required science. So, with great reluctance, I signed up for a zoology course. My instructor, Marie Tucker, was tough—but in addition to making us work hard, she also made zoology fascinating. Today when I read about DNA and genetics, I'm able to enjoy at least some comprehension thanks in part to Dana College and Marie Tucker for pushing me to expand my horizons.

It could be that the next book you read is the avenue for stretching your mind. I know almost nothing about show business, but I've had the good fortune to become acquainted with Carol Channing, the singer/actor who made "Hello Dolly" famous. She bubbles. She is enthusiastic. She has a great sense of humor: when I invited her to Southern Illinois University to do "An Evening with Carol Channing," I asked if she was bringing a pianist or if we needed to supply one. She responded, "No. I'll just sing Acapulco."

I bought her autobiography, *Just Lucky I Guess*. Having met Carol, I was confident the autobiography would be just like her. I thoroughly enjoyed the humor that popped off every page—and in the process, I also learned a little about show business. How will I ever use this knowledge? I don't know. But just as a person cannot have too many friends, a person cannot have too broad a field of knowledge. Plan a specific way to expand your knowledge. Find a need, no matter how small, and do something about it. We all need to learn to stretch ourselves.

16

VISIT A NURSING HOME

I REMEMBER WHEN MY MOTHER FELL AND BROKE A BONE IN HER back, requiring hospitalization and a stay of several weeks in a nursing home. She was in her eighties, and whenever I started to leave after visiting her, she began crying, clearly fearing she would never leave the nursing home. Her concern wasn't death but that she saw so many residents who were feeble and mentally deteriorated. Fortunately for my mother, after she recovered she returned home and lived several more years.

Studies of deterioration show that lack of mental and physical exercise can play a significant role in how quickly mental and physical abilities start to worsen. When you visit residents in a nursing home, it not only brightens someone's day, but the stimulation you provide can help prolong and preserve mental faculties. Plan to visit a nursing home in your area, either by yourself or with an organization with which you are affiliated. Experienced volunteer Terry Gump recommends: "First look at your calendar to see when you have time available. Next call a nursing home and ask if they could use your help on that day. You can be specific, telling them exactly what you had in mind, or ask them what they need. Then make your choice as to what to do."

Your visit doesn't have to include some elaborate preplanned activity. It can be as simple as chatting for a while, applying polish to someone's fingernails, or reading a chapter from a favorite book. In some cases, bringing in a friendly dog can raise morale (but check with the staff first to make sure dogs are welcome). You could recruit your church choir or high school chorus to perform at the nursing home. Depending on the nature of the facility, your child or grandchild could accompany you on your visit. Many of the elders are grandparents, or at least wish they were grandparents. This can be a positive learning experience for both your child and the resident. Bring flowers from your garden and help residents make arrangements to brighten up their rooms. Even just flashing a friendly smile to all those you meet helps. It costs you nothing, but may just make someone's day. Days in a nursing home can be deadly dull and start to blend together. You can help change that.

17

IF YOU'RE IN BUSINESS . . .

FOR SEVERAL YEARS, I PUBLISHED SMALL WEEKLY NEWSPAPERS. I started with one small newspaper, gradually built it up and then acquired others, eventually using four printing plants. This certainly doesn't make me an expert on business practices, but I did learn a few things back then and through observation since then:

• Be fair to your customers and they'll be loyal to you. You may lose a dollar or two by bending over backwards for your customers, but it pays off in the long run.

• If you promise to do something, do it.

• The most successful business people are those who see the bigger picture and are willing to invest in a better community and world. Two of the wealthiest people in the nation are Warren Buffett and Bill Gates. Warren Buffett, who has a strong social conscience, is a big advocate of helping the impoverished, and Bill Gates has contributed a lot to helping libraries and assisting with health problems in Africa, among other things. Is it a coincidence that two people who are so successful also take a keen interest in the bigger picture and try to help people? Of course not.

• Be fair to your employees. This can include basic things like providing healthcare protection, but also may involve more complicated assists like profit sharing.

• Work hard and your employees are likely to do the same.

• When you are faced with having to discharge an employee, do it as soon as you have made a solid decision. If possible, let him or her know toward the end of the workday, so the employee doesn't have to sit and ruminate over problems. Also, allow for time to spend with the person, explaining why you are letting him or her go. Offer to assist as he or she looks for new employment. This is sometimes more difficult than it sounds, but it's usually very appreciated.

In sum: Work with your employees; be willing to make the tough decisions; help your employees but also help the much larger world beyond your business.

18

SELECT A DEVELOPING NATION
AND BECOME INFORMED ABOUT IT

SURVEYS SHOW THAT AMERICANS RANK DEAD LAST AMONG western nations when it comes to knowledge of geography. In 2000, a Gallup Poll of young people reported "an appallingly low awareness of facts related to world events and leaders."[16] Pick a nation outside of western Europe, Japan, and Canada that you want to learn more about. It might be Guatemala or Liberia or Botswana or Myanmar or Albania or any of the other almost 180 developing countries. Start a file where you can keep information about that country. Include any articles you've read from newspapers or magazines. Write to its ambassador to the United States in Washington, D. C., and to the U.S. ambassador in that country and request information. Research on the Internet and at your local library. Look up information in an encyclopedia. Become familiar with the country: its people, culture, history, problems, and potential. This will inevitably lead you to learn something about the countries that border it—and suddenly you're on your way to being better informed than most Americans when it comes to geography.

We tend to focus our interest on western Europe, probably because many of us have family ties there, however remote they may be. We feel cultural connections to that part of the world. But we should also pay more attention to the impoverished areas, because it is politically important for the United States and, from a humanitarian viewpoint, we should give opportunity to the poor of the world. Our insensitivity to other nations is sometimes interpreted as arrogance. Robert MacNeil, former co-host of the *MacNeil-Lehrer News Hour,* observes in his recent partial autobiography, *Looking for My Country,* that the United States "seems to outsiders to admire itself excessively."[17] Few who travel beyond our borders would dispute that statement.

Once you gain some knowledge and understanding of these countries—or of the one nation you select—you will feel a responsibility to respond to their food and water problems and to persuade the United States to feel an obligation to work with other nations to provide aid and prevent armed conflict within their borders.

For example, Liberia, which has more historic ties to the United States than any other African nation, has been fighting a bloody civil war—adding to the woes of a country in which the capital city has neither a water nor an electrical system. Why am I concerned about Liberia? Probably because I have visited there three times. I've seen the challenges that they face. I don't want the United States to turn its back on Africa. Too many presidents and secretaries of state have ignored this immense continent and all of its problems and potential. I don't know who persuaded President George W. Bush to make his trip to Africa, but to the president's credit he went, which helped him better understand these countries and their people.

Visiting a country can give you firsthand insight and also help promote understanding. Figure out what a trip to the nation you select would cost, and start saving a few dollars each week, if possible, in an account set aside for that purpose. If saving for a trip is beyond your means—but make sure it really is—the next best thing is to find someone from that country you can exchange E-mail or letters with, or perhaps even better, arrange for students in a school near you to exchange E-mail or letters with a similar age group in "your country." You should be able to coordinate this through the American embassy in that country. If you write to a U.S. embassy in another nation and do not get a response, contact your local senator or representative's office, and they should be able to help you.

As you accumulate knowledge and become familiar with a developing nation—particularly if you're able to travel there—you will change from being indifferent to that nation's problems to becoming a passionate advocate. Inevitably you will be asking yourself: What can we do to help these people, to give them more of the same opportunities that we have? We desperately need such advocates.

19

Learn Another Language (or at Least a Few Phrases of It)

Whenever I encounter someone with a Polish name and a heavy accent, I try one of the few Polish phrases I know and usually there is a big smile greeting me. Whenever I see someone using sign language, I greet them in one of the few phrases in sign that I know and I receive the same pleased response. Reaching out internationally with language is more and more important. It's a small recognition of another culture. It is true that in the field of commerce, English is more and more widely spoken. But it is also true that a decreasing percentage of the world's population speaks English. Even better than learning a few phrases is taking the time to acquire rudimentary skills in that language, ideally followed by a trip to a nation that speaks it.

We are the only nation where one can earn a PhD and never study another language. We are also the only nation where you can take two years of French (or any language) and say, "I have studied French." And as far as I have found, we are the only nation where you are not required to study another language in grade school. A small minority of grade schools, high schools, and colleges require foreign language study, but it is indeed a tiny minority. This is one of the reasons for our insensitivity to other countries.

After September 11th, the U.S. intelligence agencies and the Defense Department scurried to find people who could speak Arabic and also pass security screening tests. At least two

American deaths occurred in Iraq, after the President said hostilities had ended, because of lack of Arabic language skills. When the Soviet Union still existed, the CIA received newspapers from many Soviet areas—but didn't have anyone to translate some of the papers.

You can aid the cause of international understanding through language study:

• Find out what foreign language opportunities exist in your community for someone in kindergarten or first grade, ideally as a starter, but also for older ages. You might want to attend these classes.

• If you can afford it, send your child or grandchild to a language camp for a week or two of intensive study (residential camps usually require a minimum age of eight). The most widely known language camp in the United States is at Concordia College in Moorhead, Minnesota, but there are others. Colleges that emphasize language study are scattered across the country from the Monterey Institute in California to Middlebury College in Vermont.

• If you can afford it, send your college-age son or daughter or nephew or niece or grandchild to study abroad for a summer or a semester. They can learn so much from studying abroad, particularly in the developing nations. Getting to know the international students attending our colleges also provides a great opportunity for our students and for us, too.

• Adults can increase their business or academic standing by studying abroad, even for a short period. And if there is no economic gain, there will definitely be a cultural one.

• Find some language tapes—either for sale or perhaps on loan from your library. You can learn the basics of another language listening to these tapes.

• Contact your school board members and urge them to join the small list of quality elementary schools that require foreign language study. Only 7 percent of our elementary school students now take foreign language courses.

• Write a letter to the editor of the local newspaper, explaining why your community should be enriched and your children enlightened by requiring foreign language study.

We hear again and again, "The world is getting smaller." Simply mouthing that trite reality does nothing to help your children's or the nation's future. Learning a foreign language assists in the economically important area of foreign trade, aids in security, promotes understanding, and helps make the world a smaller place.

20

ENCOURAGE VOLUNTEERS
FOR OVERSEAS ASSIGNMENTS—
OR TAKE ONE YOURSELF

NOTHING IS MORE EXHILARATING THAN ENCOUNTERING American volunteers in a remote village in Africa or Asia or Latin America. They may be Peace Corps workers; volunteers with a religiously affiliated group like the Mormons, who do their two-year missions; Red Cross workers; or Americans working with a foreign-based organization like the French-initiated Doctors Without Borders. All are contributing, making a good impression for our nation, and as the volunteers will tell you, returning to the United States with a better understanding of the rest of the world.

It might not be realistic for you to devote a year or two to something like the Peace Corps, but there are short-term projects organized by religious and charitable foundations that use volunteers. Volunteers with medical backgrounds are especially appreciated, but carpenters, people who sew, plumbers, and teachers are needed, too. Lillian Carter, the mother of President Jimmy Carter, joined the Peace Corps when she was sixty-eight years old—several years before her son's presidential inauguration. She became a great spokesperson for understanding India and its people. If she can do that at the age of sixty-eight, many of you reading this can do the same.

Participants of the Marion Medical Mission, in Marion, Illinois, pay their own way to Malawi and Tanzania and build water wells for villages that have unsafe water sources. People volunteer to spend a short time—usually a few weeks—in these villages. This group has no paid staff, they're all volunteers, and donations go entirely toward supplies for wells. I have yet to meet a participant who didn't feel inspired by the experience.

In 2002, Congress voted $520 million to the J. Walter Thompson Agency for a public relations campaign focused on improving the image of the United States abroad, particularly in the Middle East and South Asia. Undersecretary of State Charlotte Beers testified to a Congressional committee that "a poor perception of the United States leads to unrest, and unrest has proven to be a threat to our national and international security."[18]

I'm not opposed to improving our public image, but I believe that a Peace Corps worker in a small village in Senegal does far more good than a slick public relations campaign. Without showing more interest in helping people around the globe and displaying a genuine concern about their difficulties, public relations gimmicks will have an extremely limited impact. Our public image will improve through changes in our conduct and our attitudes, not through television and radio commercials.

Using your time and resources to benefit an international effort can give you the satisfaction of helping impoverished people and the understanding of another culture. This helps our nation become more sensitive to the rest of the world, which is an area of deficiency where we need significant improvement.

21

DON'T DUCK YOUR CIVIC
RESPONSIBILITIES

AMERICAN CITIZENS ARE PRIVILEGED TO HAVE MANY RIGHTS and freedoms, but too often we take these rights for granted. To take full advantage of these rights, all citizens should, at the minimum: 1) Be informed, read about the issues, 2) Vote, 3) Volunteer to help a candidate, and 4) Write letters voicing your views to key officials.

To begin, follow the issues. Thirty-eight percent of adult Americans do not regularly read a newspaper, which means they likely are poorly informed about national and international issues. Ideally you should read more than one newspaper and more than one news magazine. Then exercise your rights. Billions of people around the globe would like to have the right to select their country's officials—and too often we assume, as Americans, that our opportunity to vote will always be there. A muscle unused diminishes in strength. Democracy's muscles also can diminish.

If there's a school board election or a city council race, don't be part of the 80 percent of the electorate that doesn't vote in local elections or part of the 50 percent that doesn't vote in presidential elections. The opportunity to vote isn't a right that is enjoyed by everyone in every country. Many countries have never held an election, and even in the United States, the right to vote has not always applied to everyone.

In 1957, Martin Luther King Jr. asked me to speak at the second anniversary of the bus boycott in Montgomery, Alabama. I was a green young state legislator—twenty-eight years old, the same age as Martin Luther King. I spent two days with him, Ralph Abernathy, and others in Montgomery, going to churches to explain to African Americans how to fill out the long voter registration forms that were required only of them. Whites faced no such test before being allowed to vote. Since that time I have visited several developing nations during their first voting opportunity in the history of their country. It was a responsibility their people assumed with dedication and enthusiasm. The long lines that formed before the polls even opened were unbelievable.

After September 11th, the U.S. flag was displayed in cars and windows everywhere. I'm enough of an old-fashioned patriot that I like that. I served overseas in the Army under that flag and my home in rural Illinois proudly flies the flag. But sometimes when I see a car going by with the flag prominently displayed, I want to stop the car and ask the occupants if they voted in the last election.

For those of us who have never been denied the right to vote or who haven't ever faced big hurdles in doing so, that right seems to start slipping on our personal gauge of what's important, and every year a smaller and smaller percentage of our population votes.

To get even more involved, pick a candidate whose policies you applaud and volunteer on his or her campaign. People will pay greater attention to you and your ideas if they see that you are willing to work for your convictions, not just talk about them.

At the age of fifteen, Dan Alexander of Alton High School in Illinois volunteered to go door-to-door on behalf of my bid for state representative, a campaign that most people said wouldn't succeed. They turned out to be wrong, and one of the reasons for my victory was Dan Alexander. Not only did he participate, but he persuaded other high school students to do the same. By the time he was sixteen, every political leader in Madison County knew of Dan Alexander—and listened to him. One of his high school volunteers, Bill Haine, eventually became the prosecuting attorney for the county and then a highly respected state senator. Dan not only helped candidates, he also assisted in launching the political career of Bill Haine. The small extra things that we do can create unexpected ripples that expand to improve our government and society.

Another way to get involved is to write a letter to a public official giving your view on one issue at least twice a year. In order to have the biggest impact, limit your letter to one issue, two at the most. Make the letter brief. Most people are unaware of the power they have with just one postage stamp. If one-tenth of one percent of our population wrote a letter to members of the U.S. House and Senate, urging support for or against an issue, great results can occur.

For example, in an attempt to sound "tough on crime," members of Congress and state legislators passed a mandatory minimum jail sentence, which is sending people to jail who don't need to be in jail. As a result, the United States, which makes up 4 percent of the world's population, also makes up 25 percent of the world's prisoners. Michigan's republican governor, John Engler, signed bills repealing the harshest penalties in that state for non-violent crimes during his last weeks in office. Why did Michigan's legislature (Iowa has done the same) reverse the trend for sentences that end up being costly to prisoners and costly to taxpayers? What made these two governors sign that legislation even though they risked being accused of being "soft on crime"? At least in part, the answer comes from a small number of citizens who used a powerful tool at their command, a letter, and wrote to policymakers about this folly.

In summary, if you want to really feel patriotic you should: Be informed, vote, volunteer to help a candidate, and write letters to key officials with your views.

22

Send $25 to a Candidate
You Support

LOOK FOR A CANDIDATE WHO IS WILLING TO TAKE A FEW STANDS that may not be popular, who does not simply pander to the polls. Don't expect perfection of that person—that is not the lot of humanity. Send a note with your contribution, stating (if you believe as I do) that you would like to see our system of financing campaigns changed. Nowadays, the reality is that those who have the most money almost always win elections, and generally, those who have the most money got it because they're willing to do favors for the big campaign contributors. This practice distorts our system of government, making it less responsive to those with great needs, both at home and abroad. Your contribution lets candidates know that you want independence from the big con-tributors. It is a message that shows you care, and all of us—politicians and non-politicians—tend to listen more intently to those who care.

When you fill out your income tax form, you have the option to make a $3 contribution to the Presidential Election Campaign Fund, which is meant to help reduce candidates' dependence on large contributions from individuals and groups and helps to place each candidate on an equal financial level in the general election. The $3 is a signal to an officeholder or a candidate that people are paying attention to what is happening. It's a vote for a president to perform with independence from the usual campaign sources.

The illness of campaign financing in our democracy doesn't just exist at the presidential level, but electing a chief executive who acts with independence and courage can be a buffer against other campaign finance abuses.

John Brademas, an outstanding member of Congress and more recently retired as president of New York University, says in his first race for the U.S. House he spent $15,000 and lost by one-half of 1 percent. Two years later he ran and won, but each year the cost of campaigning grew at a rate much higher than inflation. In 1980 he lost, spending $675,000. In 2002, the Democratic candidate in that district spent $1.3 million and the Republican spent $1.8 million. And there are other examples throughout the nation more dramatic than that.

Imagine if you learned that a teacher at your child's college is accepting financial gifts from a student in a class of one hundred—and that instructor is going out of his or her way to do favors (like good grades) for that student. You would be rightfully outraged.

This is not unlike how our system of financing campaigns works today. A fraction of 1 percent of the population contributes almost all the money to political campaigns, and too often the laws are written to benefit that fraction of 1 percent.

You can help change that.

23

ATTEND A SCHOOL BOARD MEETING

YOUR LOCAL CITY COUNCIL OR VILLAGE BOARD PROBABLY attracts a small gathering at each meeting, people who are there to discuss complaints about a hole in the street or the size of a water bill or the need to have a traffic light at a corner. All of these are important. But the school board meeting, which deals with the future of our children, rarely draws in more than a handful of visitors, and often not even that. Unless you are in an unusual situation, the school board has much more to do with the future of your family than the city council. And unless you are an unusual citizen, you probably can't name two members of your local school board. Show an interest in the future of your children and grandchildren and other children in your city or community. This can make a real difference!

Are the people on the school board, who are planning your child's future, concerned, quality, and responsible citizens? If you can't answer that question, or, if after attending a meeting you answer the question in the negative, maybe you should consider becoming a candidate for the school board or recruiting a good candidate. Your school isn't going to drift into becoming a better school. It'll take tough decisions and strong leadership—that maybe you can help provide.

In addition to visiting a school board meeting, another effective way to ground yourself in what our schools should be doing is to read the booklet, "The Civic Mission of Schools." It is the product of approximately fifty thoughtful leaders, most of them are not from the field of education. You can receive a copy by writing to the Carnegie Corporation of New York, 437 Madison Avenue, New York, New York 10022, or you can download a copy at www.civicmissionofschools.org.

Taking five minutes to obtain that booklet could mean a big difference for your local schools and for the future of your children and young people in your community.

24

Become a Giraffe!

Ann Medlock worked as a well-paid writer for New York advertising agencies. She heard a talk given by Joseph Campbell, a teacher at Sarah Lawrence College, who spoke of the need for people to do constructive things to build a better society. Ann decided she wanted to do something more meaningful with her life. She began by interviewing people who had stuck their necks out to do good things. She called them "Giraffes." Soon she started the Giraffe Project, and she incorporated it in 1984. Now there are participants in all fifty states and sixty-two foundations that support its endeavors.

When I heard about the Giraffe Project from Nancy Jackson, an enthusiastic Illinois elementary school teacher, my first thought was: "We need a Giraffe Project (or Giraffe Caucus) in Congress, people who are willing to stick out their necks to help others." Courage is the quality most needed, but each of us can be a Giraffe. Here are four examples:

In 1975, three devout Christians bought a secluded farm in Annapolis, California, where they could live in peace and prayer. But the Starcross Community's serenity didn't last long, once they stuck their necks out to take in babies with AIDS.

There was serious community opposition, but they went on to open an AIDS outreach center in neighboring Santa Rosa.

They've so completely given up their secluded lives that they're even helping AIDS babies in Romania.

The members of the Starcross Community are Giraffes.

Gail Story of Bumpass Cove, Tennessee, was living a quiet life—keeping house, raising children. The children got sick a lot and that worried her. Then she discovered why they were getting sick—a toxic waste dump was poisoning their water.

Gail recruited her neighbors to stand in the road with her, blocking the dump trucks.

After they got that dump closed, Gail stuck her neck out to help other communities do the same thing.

Gail Story is a Giraffe.

Samuel Hightower is a painting contractor in Boston. That's his business. But his passion is helping poor kids study music.

Sam has invested all of his savings and spare time in this dream. He recruits Boston area musicians to teach—and neighborhood kids to learn.

He can't afford fancy buildings and equipment, but dozens of kids are making music now, thanks to one determined Giraffe, Sam Hightower.

In 1983, Ray Buchanan and Ken Horne of Big Island, Virginia, made a discovery—potato farmers destroy potatoes that aren't the exact size and shape grocery stores want. Perfectly healthy, tasty potatoes. With so many hungry people in our country, that didn't seem right.

So Ray and Ken stuck out their necks and started the Potato Project, getting this good food to people who needed it. They've moved hundreds of millions of pounds of potatoes to hungry people in forty-seven states.

Ray Buchanan and Ken Horne are Giraffes.[19]

Ann Medlock continues to inspire a host of Giraffes. We can learn from Ann Medlock's example. To learn more about the Giraffe Project write to: P. O. Box 759, Langley, WA 98260, or contact them at www.giraffe.org.

Become a Giraffe! Once a month for three months, take a chance for a good cause—stick out your neck. Be willing to risk a little embarrassment or time or money. Write down the courageous thing you do each month in a diary, if you keep one, or on a sheet of paper. Put the paper under some clothes in a drawer. You may forget about it temporarily—but when you come across it later, you'll reread it and relive the satisfaction of being a Giraffe, and more than likely you'll want to repeat that experience.

25

DON'T BE TOO PESSIMISTIC

SOME PEOPLE LOOK AT THE DARK SIDE OF EVERYTHING, AND with rare exceptions, they don't do much that is constructive. We all have shortcomings—individually and collectively—but the people who improve things and get things done are not the naysayers. Tennyson wrote:

> Ah, what shall I be at fifty,
> Should nature keep me alive,
> If I find the world so bitter,
> When I am but twenty-five?

People quickly tire of constant complainers. It's not good for the complainer and not good for everyone else. Bitterness is like cancer; it eats away at you. Ask yourself if your attitude is positive. If an honest evaluation suggests an excessively gloomy look at things on your part, try for one hour to be positive. The next day make it two hours. Do what you can not to become a naysayer. Be realistic, of course, but look at the brighter side of things more frequently. You will surprise yourself.

Gordon Allen of Eldorado, Illinois, is eighty-eight years old. Whenever anyone refers to Gordon, it's almost always accompanied by a comment like, "Isn't he a great guy?" Always ready with a smile, Gordon's also always ready to help with whatever good cause needs assistance. He holds no titles, but he has enthusiasm and warmth and a positive attitude.

Each month, *Woman's Day* magazine has a section that's titled, "How to Change the World." The readers of the magazine are not the U.S. president and his cabinet, nor the heads of major businesses, but rather ordinary citizens the magazine recognizes who have the potential to change the world.

USA Weekend, the weekly newspaper supplement, has a similar program. It sponsors "Make a Difference Day." *USA Weekend* asks newspapers around the nation to get their readers to act, and more than five hundred newspapers participate. It has resulted in everything from helping an orphanage in Laredo, Texas, to "literacy parties" sponsored by Altrusa International, a service organization; from teenagers cleaning up trash in Goshen, California, to nine-year-old Ryan Fosnow in Mundelein, Illinois, collecting crayons and other supplies for students from low-income families who can't afford them.

The people who get things done—whether nine years old or ninety—are not the pessimists. Pessimists are people who give up easily, and no one conquers obstacles to good deeds by giving up. Believe that you can make a difference, and you will.

26

VISIT SOMEONE IN PRISON OR JAIL— OR HELP IN SOME OTHER WAY

YOU PROBABLY DON'T HAVE TO ASK AROUND TOO FAR BEFORE you discover a friend or relative of yours or of someone you know who is serving time. More than 2.2 million Americans are in prison or jail. Most people in prison eventually will be let out. There is a lot that can be done for prisoners while they are incarcerated: improve their education, teach them job skills, and just let them know there are people who care about them. Some prisoners are so deeply scarred emotionally that assisting them isn't easy, but there are also many others who respond to simple gestures of interest and concern, giving them a spark of hope that could turn their lives around.

Charles Colson went from the high of being a key adviser to President Richard Nixon to the low of spending time in a federal prison. But he decided to use his difficult experience and new insights to help others. He formed Prison Fellowship, a religiously oriented group that helps those incarcerated, and has given hope to many men and women who before had none.

Another organization, Prisoner Visitation and Support, has trained several hundred volunteers to visit prisoners. For more information or to become a volunteer, contact them at 1501 Cherry Street, Philadelphia, PA 19102, (215) 241-7117, or visit their Web site at www.prisonervisitation.org.

Most people, however, are not going to take this training. But the lack of it shouldn't deter you from volunteering to visit prisons. If you feel awkward visiting someone, take a small first step by sending a paperback book to someone you know, or send several books to the jail or prison to be distributed to prisoners who may be interested. Most jails and prisons do not accept hardcover books, and make sure the books you send are uplifting, or at least informative or entertaining. No murder mysteries!

Paroled gang members are more than twice as likely to return to prison as non-gang members. Gang members in prison are also:

• more likely than other prisoners to have not completed high school.

• less likely to have had a job before going to prison and less likely to have one upon discharge from prison, or during probation.

• more apt to have a history of illegal drug abuse.

It's important to try to discourage young men (and a few young women) from joining gangs in the first place. Find out what is being done in the impoverished neighborhoods in your area to encourage school attendance and to help those who are struggling, both at home and at school. Help one teenager to find a meaningful part-time job. Volunteer to be a mentor to a young person. Check on the effectiveness of the drug treatment and education programs in your community. These are preventive measures that can help our nation's youth and protect our society.

It's not possible to tackle all of the ideas mentioned in this chapter. But you can make a start by picking one, and hopefully it will stimulate you to do more.

27

HELP A PRISONER CONNECT
WITH HIS OR HER FAMILY

IT MAY SEEM LIKE I'M DEVOTING AN EXCESSIVE AMOUNT OF attention to the problems of prisoners, but let me share these grim statistics: In addition to the more than 2.2 million Americans in prisons or jails—one for every 143 citizens—another four million are under court supervision for probation or under parole limitations and guidance; more people per one hundred thousand are in U.S. prisons than any other nation; the United States has 4 percent of the world's population but 25 percent of its prisoners. Four times as many people are incarcerated today than in the mid-1970s, despite an overall drop in violent crime.

Time in prison or jail can cause estrangement from a family, a strained situation that isn't good for the prisoner or the family. Volunteers can help both the inmate and the family by recording the prisoner reading stories for his or her children. Audiotapes can help improve reading skills—which is often a major problem—and build ties between the prisoner and his or her children. The prisoner can add a personal message at the end of the recording, for example, "I miss you and love you." The county jail in McLean County (Bloomington), Illinois, runs a program like this and it's very popular with the prisoners and their families, jail officials, and the volunteers. Finding an organization to sponsor this effort and work with prison or jail officials is probably the best approach to a successful program.

By encouraging ties to the family, these volunteers can help ease the transition from prison to a life of freedom. A program like this also encourages inmates who cannot read to sign up for education programs—in those prisons that have them—which can help the prisoner's future. An article in *Atlantic Monthly* observed: "A recent study sponsored by the Virginia Department of Correctional Education, in which inmates were tracked for fifteen years, found that recidivism among those who pursued an education while in prison was 59 percent lower."[20] A study of Bedford Hills Correctional Study in New York found that the women inmates' return-to-custody rate three years after being discharged was 7.7 percent for those who participated in college training compared to the overall rate of 29.9 percent—yet the federal government has made it more difficult for prisoners to take college courses.[21]

Check with your local prison or jail to find out if it provides a reading program for its prisoners and their families. If an organization is sponsoring it, you can volunteer through that group. If, as is much more likely, no one has started a program like this, mention it to an organization to which you belong and suggest that group appoint a committee to look at the possibilities. With the right people, you can start a program that can make a really positive difference.

28

WORKING WITH OTHERS, HELP A FORMER PRISONER FIND A JOB

YEARS AGO, A MEN'S CLUB AT A CHURCH CONTACTED ME AND explained that they were looking to take on a socially sensitive project—did I have a suggestion? Coincidentally, the day before, someone who had served time in prison for embezzlement called me, desperate for a job. I told the church leader that I had just the project for them and shared with him the former prisoner's struggle. Two weeks later the church leader called back: "Do you have an easier project for us?" Applying faith to life is rarely easy.

Contact a local parole officer who can help you identify a recently released person who needs help. Get a committee of three or four people from your organization to meet, first with the parole officer, then with the former prisoner. Figure out what you can do to help assist in meeting this person's needs. I use the plural "needs," because often former prisoners are facing other challenges in addition to finding employment. For example, they may be battling an alcohol or a drug addiction problem, they may have a medical problem and can no longer afford to buy their prescriptions, they may need decent clothing so they can apply for a job and make a good impression. Everything in life can be complicated, and helping a former prisoner is no exception—but that shouldn't prevent us from doing a good deed that gives someone a chance.

There's no guarantee that your efforts will produce positive results, but with your help, this person stands a better chance of succeeding and staying out of prison. Assisting a former prisoner can be an eye-opening and learning experience for both you and the former prisoner. It can give you better insight into the hardships that some people face, and the person you're helping might feel a little more welcomed back into society, knowing that there are people who care.

29

REMEMBER THE MOST VALUABLE GIFT YOU HAVE OUTSIDE OF GOOD HEALTH IS TIME

IF YOU'LL FORGIVE MY IMMODESTY—MODESTY IS NOT A VIRTUE of most people who hold or have held public office—this is my twenty-second book. I also teach at Southern Illinois University, head a Public Policy Institute there, serve on too many boards and committees, and do a fair amount of national and international volunteer activities that frequently take me around the nation and overseas about three times a year. People occasionally ask how I do it. Here are a few of my "secrets":

I rarely schedule appointments for visitors for more than fifteen minutes; perhaps once every two weeks I schedule lunch with someone, otherwise I eat at my desk and keep working. When I travel I always take things to read as well as other work and sometimes my portable typewriter. (I realize the typewriter is slower than working on a computer—this is one of my time weaknesses—but I'm comfortable with it. I do use the computer for research.) Even on vacations I take some work with me, but I do believe taking time off to "recharge my batteries" is also important.

I set aside time for family vacations usually twice a year, getting my children and grandchildren together. Sometimes we play canasta or a game that is new to me, like Shanghai rummy. My life is not all work, but I do try to make good use of my time. And I confess, I occasionally enjoy watching football games on TV. While the time I allot to football is substantially less than other people's TV viewing, I'm sure there's a little self-delusion on my part that football is somehow a better time investment than watching soap operas or Jerry Springer.

And in my "spare time":

• I read books. Fiction generally bores me, so it's usually non-fiction.

• When I do my daily treadmill exercise, I try to watch a video that is informational. Occasionally, I work in a Marx Brothers film—not very informational but great fun.

• When I travel, I visit villages in the country where I'm speaking and also try to visit at least one other nation. I usually notify the State Department where I'm going so it can use me to lecture at a university or some other place where I might be helpful.

• I always take more work than I think I'll need when traveling, so if I get stuck in a city or an airport for a lengthy period I can use my time profitably.

• I take something to read when I have a medical appointment. There's almost always a wait, and most people waste the time they're waiting.

• I try to be punctual for all appointments so I don't waste someone else's time.

• Whenever I walk somewhere, I try to walk quickly—at the age of seventy-four I don't walk as quickly as I once did, but more quickly than most people. I believe this improves my body, probably lengthens my life, and makes me slightly more alert. If I save three minutes a day by walking rapidly, during a year I will save eighteen hours and fifteen minutes—and I can get a great deal done in eighteen hours and fifteen minutes.

I'd estimate that one-third of the time I'm on a plane the person sitting next to or across the aisle from me, does nothing but look out the window or stare ahead, or occasionally sleeps. The sleep they may require, but they don't need to waste time while they're on a plane. It's not only what they could be doing to enrich their lives, studies also show that if we keep our minds active, we're less likely to develop problems like Alzheimer's later in life.

It is only fifteen minutes from my home to my office, but during the drive I play tapes to learn more about Grover Cleveland or the American Indian "Trail of Tears" or the life of St. Augustine. It doesn't surprise me that some of the busiest and most productive people I know do the same. Tom Sullivan, a prominent Chicago lawyer and former U.S. Attorney, and Dr. James Dove, a cardiologist based in Springfield, Illinois, play tapes in their car. Tapes are available through libraries, or they can be purchased or rented through bookstores or companies that will send you a catalog and regular mailings.

One of the most successful and respected people I know wrote: "Some people don't know how to work. They dilly-dally all day. I advise getting to work at least fifteen minutes before expected and staying until your work is completed, including answering every telephone call before you leave for the day. I realized when I was in the army (I did personnel work) that my IQ was not high enough to outsmart people so I decided I could not let anyone outwork me." That formula has certainly been effective for him.

Adam Guettel is the talented grandson of composer Richard Rodgers. He laments: "I've lost a good 20 percent of my singing ability by frying my voice with alcohol and cigarettes and pot. But the big thing I've lost is time . . . conservatively ten years of writing, because it's sixteen years since I got out of school, and I was gainfully employed for only six of them."[22]

President George W. Bush is also time efficient. A 3:30 meeting will start at 3:30. He believes in "thriftiness with time." A former speech writer for him says he is conscious that "every time you let someone ramble [in a meeting] you destroy a minute."[23]

Leaders in any field find ways to use their time effectively. However, you don't need to be a leader to take advantage of that clock ticking away your life. Here is a practical suggestion: Keep a minute-by-minute time log for yourself for three days. You'll be surprised at the result. Next, plan how you can use your time more effectively.

30

DONATE TO GOOD CAUSES

THE LIST OF WORTHWHILE CAUSES IS ENDLESS. FOR EXAMPLE, those that help the world's impoverished include: CARE, Red Cross, the Heifer Project, Bread for the World, World Vision, Doctors Without Borders, Catholic Relief Services, Lutheran World Relief, Church World Service, Jewish National Fund, United Jewish Appeal—and so on. They all do exceptional work, but most Americans donate nothing or just a little to them. Even a one dollar contribution helps. Most of the groups have a tax deductible status, which can help soften the blow to your pocketbook and make it a little easier to donate. Good causes need money; they need your generosity.

Parade magazine has joined with ABC Television, American Express, Betty Crocker, Tyson Foods, and others to enlist help for an anti-poverty, anti-hunger organization called Share Our Strength, founded and headed by William Shore. It encourages businesses to share a small percentage of their profits with the poor and hungry. Parade has started an annual "American Bake Sale," urging people around the nation to have a bake sale with the proceeds going to Share Our Strength. Parade shares this story:

> Michael Duran studies his plate of turkey and green beans carefully, as if it might be a mirage. Tonight, at Denver's J. Churchill Owen Branch Boys and Girls Club, Michael, age fourteen, doesn't have to leave the dinner table until his

stomach is full. In this cheerful cafeteria with construction-paper animals winking from the walls, more than one hundred children can eat their fill for free. But for more years than he cares to remember, Michael and his younger sisters went to bed hungry.

Estranged from their father, they moved from motel to motel with their mother as she searched for odd jobs and battled a drug problem. Some nights she remembered to bring back food; more often she did not. So, from the time he was nine years old, Michael was Arayna and Ashley's lifeline.

"It's hard to talk about this," Michael says. "I'm trying to forget." For years he scavenged through convenience stores, stealing to keep himself and his sisters alive. "Mostly I took bread and bologna, whatever would make us the fullest," says Michael. "Sometimes I'd get caught, and they'd tell me I was too young to steal. But I had to get food. You won't survive if you sit still."[24]

There are people like Michael all over this nation, and many more in other nations. It would be great if Michael and his sisters could visit with you in your home. They can't, but you can reach out to them with a contribution.

Sharing will help you.

Helen Deniston of Carbondale, Illinois, relates: "Several years ago my son and I were approached by a gentleman on the steps of a pizza place asking for money for food. My son invited him in to share a pizza with us. Walking with my grandson some years later, my grandson asked me for money to buy an orange. We had just eaten and I didn't think it was necessary, but I gave it to him anyway. I was touched to see him give the orange to a person who was asking for money to buy food."

Sometimes simply giving money to someone isn't the right answer; too often the money will get used for alcohol and sometimes drugs. What Helen Deniston's son and grandson did is usually better, because you can be sure that your generosity is being used for food. Better still is to support programs that give the hungry and homeless a chance.

It's not always easy to know if you should give a small amount to many causes or concentrate your donation to one group. There is no simple answer to this. Each of us has to make our own decisions about giving. For example, I tend not to give to organizations that solicit by mail too frequently, figuring they waste too much money on raising money, and I also avoid giving to organizations that send me labels or other gimmicks, again a waste of their resources. But what is clear is that not giving and sharing is unacceptable.

31

Encourage the Arts

What is your community doing to enrich the arts in your area? When I served in the army I was stationed in Coburg, Germany, in northern Bavaria, a community of forty thousand, with perhaps sixty thousand in the county (Kreis) in which it is located. Coburg had a year-round full-time professional theater, orchestra, and opera company. Germany has fifty-seven year-round professional opera companies; the United States has none. Even the Metropolitan Opera in New York City is not year-round. Talented opera students in the United States generally have to go to Europe if they want a permanent place to live while they work.

Alert business leaders know that their companies are likely to have more stability in a community that has quality schools, a fine library, and an enriching arts program. If you see a gap in the cultural offerings of your community, write a letter to the editor of your local newspaper, recommending that someone start things rolling, and perhaps add that anyone interested should contact you. It's not likely you'll achieve in your community what Coburg has, but it usually only takes one person who's a sparkplug to get a community chorus, or an amateur theater group, or some other form of the arts started. You may be happily surprised at what you accomplish!

In addition to art galleries and plays and other traditional displays of the arts, creativity can result in fascinating ventures that can stimulate your local community and attract visitors. Paducah, Kentucky, created a National Quilt Museum. Mt. Vernon, Illinois, a city of eighteen thousand population, offers an unusually fine museum that was donated to the community by former residents. It's one of the finest small community museums in the nation. In Litchfield, Illinois, Joe Kempe, a retired printer who worked for the *St. Louis Post-Dispatch*, is developing a printing museum named "Hot Metal Heaven" for the printing process primarily used until about 1975. After his wife died he wanted something constructive to do and started this museum. It's still in its infancy, but it already has a regular newsletter. Joe Kempe is eighty-four and no one would have criticized him if he had quietly enjoyed his retirement playing golf or chess and visiting with friends in a senior citizen center. Instead he is enriching his community, and those who come to visit, with a unique museum.

While growing up in Eugene, Oregon, my parents—primarily my mother—regularly took my brother and me to concerts. We heard several of the world's greatest performers. One of the concerts I really looked forward to each year was the Eugene Gleemen, a group of about fifty local men who not only enriched our hometown audience, but they also traveled to other communities, sharing their cultural talents and creating good public relations for Eugene. I was too young to judge the quality of the singing, but I knew enough about music to really appreciate them.

Several years ago in Carbondale, Illinois, Jack and Muriel Hayward held several chamber music concerts in their living room, featuring members of the Southern Illinois University School of Music faculty and students. This small step led to the founding of the Southern Illinois Chamber Music Society, which presents an annual series of chamber music concerts and raises money to provide scholarships for students who have the ability to play in public. There's no reason scholarships should be limited to athletes. The Haywards are helping students as well as adding to the cultural life of their community.

Somewhere in the United States a community similar to the one where I live—a rural area with a university town of twenty-six thousand as its hub—will decide that one way to attract tourists and industry is to build a culturally rich region. An arts district will be formed and possibly a small tax to fund the arts will be implemented—perhaps one cent per gallon of gas or ten cents per pack of cigarettes—and soon that community will offer concerts, plays, lectures at the university, and perhaps also a full-time professional orchestra or other such ventures that will instill pride to local people, and attract tourism dollars and businesses that want their employees to have a fine cultural opportunity.

Maybe you're the one to start stimulating people with this idea. Once it happens in one community, it'll be like dropping a stone in a quiet lake; the ripples will continue to reach out and out.

32

LISTEN TO PEOPLE

PEOPLE LIKE TO TALK ABOUT THEMSELVES. A FEW BASIC QUESTIONS can usually start a healthy conversation: Where were you born? Where did you go to school? What do you do? Do you have a family? Soon you're likely to "connect" about mutual friends or places or interests. But sometimes one of the hardest things to do is listen. And if, like me, you have a hearing impairment (I've worn hearing aids for about ten years), you may have to ask people to do things like spell their last names. People usually don't mind doing that.

Terry and Woody Gump are two very likeable people. She's a speech therapist and Woody is a civil engineer, retired from the Illinois Department of Transportation. Terry recalls: "One of the first reunions we attended of my class at Lincoln Christian College in Lincoln, Illinois, was after two of our children had arrived. I will never forget it. It was there that my husband ever so gently taught me to focus on others. The college had planned several days of events, starting on a Thursday evening and ending with a banquet on Saturday evening. I remember how excited I was to get to tell others about our children, where we were living, and what we were doing. After we arrived at our motel room, Woody and I started talking about the events of that evening. He said, 'I noticed that you seemed excited to tell others about our kids, our plans, and our activities, but I didn't notice you asking about their families and activities.' Confronting someone you love with something like this is not always easy. I'm glad Woody did this in private and did it after the first evening. For the rest of the reunion I remembered his words. I made it a point to ask about other classmates' families and asked to see their pictures. Since I brought pictures of my own, and enjoyed showing them, I knew others might have brought pictures, too, and would most likely want to show them. Asking others about themselves made the reunion much more enjoyable to me. How thankful I am to Woody for noticing this and telling me."

We routinely ask, "How are you?" If you don't mean it, don't ask. An alternative greeting that is sometimes a little more genuine is "Good to see you." If you do ask, listen to the person's answer, and if he or she has a problem, ask yourself if there's any way you can help. If you really listen and become more sensitive to the problems of other people, you sometimes may discover a tragedy—a death or a serious illness or an accident—that someone has experienced. Ask yourself, "What would I want others to do if this happened to me?"Then follow through. It may be bringing food, running an errand, picking up children after school, or offering to do the laundry or the dishes.

You may be familiar with the singing group Peter, Paul, and Mary. Peter is Peter Yarrow. He not only sings, he listens. He noticed that children are sometimes cruel to other children without meaning to be. If a child is fat, or has a limp or misshapen ear or burn mark on the face, other children are not likely to be silent about it. Because Peter Yarrow is sensitive, he founded Operation Respect, which developed the "Don't Laugh at Me" Program, which teaches children to respect one another. The centerpiece of the program is the song "Don't Laugh at Me," sung by Peter, Paul, and Mary. Children are being helped because Peter Yarrow listens. For more information about Operation Respect, write to: 2 Penn Plaza, 5th Floor, New York, New York 10121 or go to www.dontlaugh.org. Listening is so important.

33

HELP PRESERVE YOUR COMMUNITY'S HISTORY

MANY WHO VISIT OUR NATION SAY THAT WE ARE SUFFERING from "historical amnesia." Check with your local librarians to determine whether the local historical society or department of history at a nearby college or university has recorded the recollections of some of your community's older citizens. If nothing has been recorded, select three senior citizens in your area to interview. They will likely be eager to tell their story, even though initially they may say, "There's nothing special about my life." You will discover things that are special.

Even the smallest communities have people with rich backgrounds. Interview former mayors, school teachers, and school superintendents. The oldest citizens in your area should be recorded before it's too late. The number of veterans who served during World War II is diminishing rapidly, so, too, is the number of those who lived through the war as civilians. Most citizens will be happy to cooperate.

Prepare your questions in advance but don't be afraid to explore topics that come up during the interview. At a minimum, tape record your conversation. Even better, videotape it. Fifty years from now, people will be interested in seeing the clothing, the pictures on the wall, the little things we hardly notice today. If you have time, transcribe the recorded words into a small document that others can read. Give the final product to your local library, and also share it with the local newspaper and historical society. Encourage them to inspire others to do the same. From that small start you can help preserve the heritage of your community, enrich life for someone who looks at the transcript or watches and listens to the recording twenty years from now, and present insight into how we became the nation we are today. Others will follow your example.

34

LEARN FROM SUCCESSFUL LEADERSHIP

SELECT THREE PEOPLE FROM YOUR COMMUNITY OR YOUR field of interest who are influential and respected, who you consider to be a leader. Write each of their names at the top of a sheet of paper. Carry these sheets of paper with you for two days and whenever you think of a quality that one or all of them have, jot it down on the proper page. You'll generally discover that these people don't have more ability than you, so what makes them influential? Thirty-two years ago I wrote: "I know of no one who has genuinely tried to influence government policy, and has been willing to work at it, who has not been at least partially successful." More than three decades later, I still don't know of an exception to this rule. And it also applies to the PTA, a Rotary Club, or any other group with which you are affiliated.

If you know any of these leaders personally or if you feel comfortable, ask them what they regard as the key to effective leadership. They may have to reflect for a moment, but you'll probably get a good answer.

Convince yourself to do at least one interview. Even if you don't know the person well enough to casually approach him or her, do it anyway. Most people you ask for an interview will be pleased, because it implies they are an effective leader—and who doesn't like a compliment?

Neil Dillard, the former mayor of Carbondale, Illinois, served for four terms and probably could have served a fifth. What makes him so respected? (He may disagree with this assessment.) He isn't a great public speaker and is probably average for a public official, but citizens know he is honest, hard-working, competent, and tries to be fair to everyone. As mayor, he attended an amazing number of meetings, everything from eighth-grade plays to senior citizens' meetings. Working with the city council and city manager, he knew how to get things done. When concerned parents voiced the need for a new high school building/complex, he helped put together the package that made the building a reality, committing the city to provide $800,000 to the project over a period of years. His wife also has a great personality, though a little more outgoing than her somewhat shy husband. She attended almost as many events as he did. They make a great team. That is one public official.

Mary Cavey, a teacher at Spry Elementary School in Chicago, a school with serious problems, became its principal and helped turn things for the better. She observed, "What I learned about leadership is, never accept no for an answer."[25]

Illinois state senator Ralph Dunn, now retired, broke with his GOP party to support an increase in the state income tax for education in 1989. An unassuming lawmaker, Ralph Dunn frequently displayed courage and independence.

You pick your three leaders and make your notes. You can learn from all three.

35

REFLECT, PRAY, OR DREAM

As you're riding in a car, plane, train, or bus, reflect on your talents and needs that are so easily ignored. Reflection can be a form of prayer. But be careful with prayer. Genuine prayer usually involves a commitment. Imagine someone sitting on his front porch looking at his lawn that needs to be mowed. He is praying that the lawn be mowed—but he keeps sitting there. Something is wrong with that prayer!

I know of people who pray for world peace, who pray for the world's hungry, who pray for better government, but they just sit there. Something is wrong with those prayers, too. Prayer and reflection can be opportunities to ask for help for others, but they're also opportunities to motivate a person to act.

Take two hours from your day to sit down with a pen and paper, and ask yourself what you want to contribute to others during your life. Do some dreaming. What would you really like to be doing in ten years? Are your dreams focused mostly on you or do you see yourself in a role helping others? Write down your dreams and what steps you can take to accomplish them. Keep in mind that satisfaction in life comes from helping others. After you have your thoughts clarified, ask someone whose judgment you trust—someone who gets things done—what he or she thinks of your ideas or would suggest that could help you turn them into a reality.

As you dream and plan, recognize that changes in your life and changes in technology will alter your path to those dreams. I recently attended a dinner honoring Lou Bocardi, retired president of the Associated Press. When he started in the news business, teletypes transmitted sixty-seven words a minute to give newspapers and other news outlets the latest developments. Today, news can be transmitted at the rate of ninety-six thousand words a minute. But Lou's dreams for accuracy and balance in reporting are as pertinent today as in the sixty-seven-words-a-minute day.

By taking two hours to write about and reflect on your dreams, you'll become more focused. The words you record can change your life—not dramatically, but in small ways that are important. A slight shift in direction for a ship crossing the Atlantic determines whether the ship will land in Denmark or Portugal. If you were to observe two ships on the ocean, one with a sense of direction, the other without, the two ships will look the same, but there's a huge difference between them. Similarly, if you were to observe two people, one with a sense of direction and the other without, they will look the same, but the end results will be dramatically different. A small shift in your direction can mean the difference between a life lived with purpose or a well-intentioned but directionless life. Those two hours can help you choose.

36

DON'T SAY, "THAT WOULDN'T DO
ANY GOOD"

AGAIN AND AGAIN I'VE SEEN PEOPLE ACCOMPLISH THINGS THAT others said couldn't be done. Most major feats start out small, with unnoticed actions that seem to come out of nowhere. For instance, let me give you an example of a project I'm working on now that was inspired by two people who seem like unlikely candidates to launch such a project. I believe it will result in constructive action, but there's no certainty it will. We can't wait on certainties to do good things.

During my years in public service I've received hundreds of letters from prisoners, and through years of experience, I feel pretty confident in gauging whether a prisoner is telling me the truth or giving me a "snow job." The letter I received from Robert Felton Jr. sounded genuine and made a good impression. He is incarcerated at the Tamms State Prison in Illinois, and he read about my concern with our justice system and the high numbers in our prisons. I also received a letter from Lois Hayward, the activist wife of a retired faculty member at Southern Illinois University, urging me to visit the Tamms prison on the basis of some things she had heard. So I did.

Robert Felton Jr., perhaps thirty years old, was in isolation and reading Churchill and Lincoln, books I wish my students at the university were reading. He was in isolation because of minor mental health problems that were not treated until recently. When

I contacted the Illinois Department of Corrections Director Don Snyder about Felton, he told me that for eighteen months Robert Felton's conduct has been good—roughly the same time he has received help for his mental health problems. When I asked Felton what he eventually wanted to do after he's released from prison, he replied he wanted to become a counselor. Then he added, "I want to study to take my GED [high school equivalency] test." Because statistics show that prisoners who have a high school diploma are less likely to return to prison, I thought his request should be honored and I told that to the prison officials who were with me. The woman in charge of counseling agreed. I turned to the warden and asked, "Why can't he study for a GED and take the test?" The warden responded, to my amazement, "We have a waiting list in Illinois prisons to study for the GED." I say "to my amazement" because encouraging prisoners to study for a GED and take the exam will save lives and money for Illinois taxpayers.

Since my visit, I've talked to an aide to our governor and to Senator Barack Obama, the chair of the state senate committee that has jurisdiction, about this. I believe we will change this situation—all because one prisoner and one concerned woman wrote to me. It would have been easy for both of them to say to themselves, "Why waste my time on a letter? That wouldn't do any good." Instead they acted, and Illinois probably will become a better state as a result.

As one experienced observer notes: "Chief among the obstacles [to getting things done] is the mistaken belief that anyone who takes a committed public stand, or at least an effective one, has to be a larger-than-life figure—someone with more time, energy, courage, vision, or knowledge than a normal person could ever possess."[26] It's the little things we do that can really make a difference.

Deborah Maurer is another example of someone who did an extra little thing that may result in something you'll hear about down the road. She bought a copy of a book I wrote, *Freedom's Champion: Elijah Lovejoy*. It's the story of a leader of the anti-slavery movement before the Civil War who was killed by a mob for his strong stand. It's the most exciting book I've written. However, few people have ever heard of Elijah Lovejoy. As a result, sales have been modest. The last time I saw U. N. ambassador and former Illinois governor Adlai Stevenson before his death, he said, "Someone should make a movie out of that story." I agreed, but I don't know anything about the film business, so I did nothing to pursue the idea.

Deborah Maurer also doesn't know anything about the film business. She lives in Freeburg, Illinois, a small suburban/rural community of about four thousand citizens, and works for American Water Works in Alton, Illinois. After reading my Lovejoy book she came to the same conclusion as Adlai Stevenson. She talked to her father in Los Angeles, and repeated—with conviction—the idea about making a movie. Her father, John Townsend, isn't in the movie business either, but one day, while eating in a small restaurant in Los Angeles, he noticed another patron busily working on a document. "He's nosy," Deborah says with a laugh, describing her father. Townsend asked the gentleman what he did. It turned out the hard-working person was screenwriter Ken O'Donnell. Townsend told him about his daughter's movie idea. O'Donnell gave Townsend his business card and told him to have his daughter contact him, never expecting much to happen out of it. Deborah bought another copy of the book and sent it to O'Donnell. The screenwriter's version is that Townsend "bugged me for five minutes and I agreed to look at the book." Now O'Donnell is working on a script for a movie, has signed a contract with my publisher for movie rights, and maybe—still a maybe—a movie will be produced that can influence people in our nation and other nations about race relations and free speech. If it happens, credit will go to Deborah Maurer for initiating the project. Ken O'Donnell plans to spend much of next year writing the script and persuading a few key investors that the movie can sell. The movie's still not a reality, but it's much closer than it was a year ago, thanks to Deborah Maurer and her father.

For someone with no connections to the film industry to talk about producing a movie, it's a real long shot. Deborah Maurer easily could have said, "That wouldn't do any good," and done nothing. That's the easy way out—the way many of us take too often.

37

HELP CREATE A SENSE
OF COMMUNITY

ROBERT PUTNAM, THE KEEN OBSERVER OF OUR CULTURE, notes: "Most Americans today feel vaguely and uncomfortably disconnected."[27]

I spent twenty-two years in the Washington, D. C.–area, most of it in the city. About one of five weekends I stayed in Washington. When I walked to church on Sunday I made a point to say "hello" to everyone I encountered. Frequently people would give me a puzzled look, but soon I saw them a second or third time and they would respond with a greeting. I wanted our neighborhood to have a greater sense of community. Occasionally I would meet the same people in a grocery store and would get a warm greeting. Did I create a greater sense of community? I don't know. But there's a good chance that in a small way I did. In a small community this greeting exchange happens with ease, but if you live in a large metropolitan area, it's different. There you may be able to help create a sense of community.

The other day I took a taxi in Chicago. My cab driver, Majed Rahman, lives on 64th Street in southwest Chicago, near Midway airport. He's a Palestinian Muslim who came to the United States to give his small family opportunity and freedom. But because of his Arab and Muslim background, intrusive and uneducated people who think they're being patriotic have been throwing rocks and bricks through his windows. By the time this book is published

I hope Majed and his family will be more welcomed by their neighbors. I've been in touch with the Chicago police and the situation appears to be improving.

I grew up in Eugene, Oregon. My father served as pastor of a Lutheran church. Our ecumenical outreach was limited, and I don't remember visits to our home by Jewish rabbis or Catholic priests. When I was around ten years old, I sold *The Saturday Evening Post* for five cents each; I kept one and a half cents as a commission. One day a downpour of rain caught me. Soaked, I ducked into Rubenstein's Furniture Store to get out of the rain. I had thirty-four wet magazines that I knew no one would ever buy. Mr. Rubenstein bought all thirty-four of those magazines, an act I remember vividly to this day, and it was my first encounter with anyone in the Jewish community that I can recall. With that generous act, he helped me and helped to build a sense of community.

Small gestures can build that community spirit. Your civic organization could hold an auction and give the proceeds to the local center for abused women and children. Your church could organize a bake sale and donate the proceeds to help people in your community who have serious dental problems but can't afford to remedy them. The Newman Center (Roman Catholic), that primarily serves students at our university, provides a meal every Thanksgiving for anyone who wishes to attend. It's a grand mixture of international students, lonely U.S. students, people from the community with economic problems, and many others who fit into none of those categories. It makes everyone feel good: those who serve the food, those who donate to the meal, those who come from a near-empty campus, and local people who get acquainted with others they wouldn't ordinarily meet in the course of their normal routine. The meal helps build a sense of community.

Helping one another helps to build a sense of community. Harming one another harms everyone. With creativity, you can find small ways to help bring people together where you live.

38

LET EVERYONE KNOW WE HAVE HIGH EXPECTATIONS OF THEM, WHETHER THEY'RE IN KINDERGARTEN, COLLEGE, OR OUT OF SCHOOL

WE TEND TO LIVE UP TO PEOPLE'S EXPECTATIONS OF US. When I served as lieutenant governor of Illinois, one day my administrative assistant said, "There is a class of young students from Edwardsville in the hallway, and they would like to say hello to you." I went out and greeted them and asked, "What grade are you in?"

"The fourth grade," they responded.

Then a young boy added, "We're the dumb class." Someone—perhaps another student—conveyed something to those students that should not have been conveyed. Someone caused their expectation level to be lowered, and my guess is that their contribution to society will be less than it could be.

Habitat for Humanity's Prison Partnership program offers prisoners the opportunity to volunteer with Habitat to participate in various aspects of house construction. One of the things the founder, Millard Fuller, stresses again and again: "We are building so much more than houses. We are building people."[28] How inspiring for a prisoner—or anyone—to hear that he or she is doing something that constructive!

I once heard an angry parent say to her son, "You'll never amount to anything." What he did to cause that burst of anger I don't recall, but I know that her manner of dealing with it was wrong. What's true of young people is true of others. Testify before a congressional committee and give them no noble ideas, the legislation that may emerge will reflect that. Testify before them and tell them they have the opportunity to make a huge contribution to the nation and outline a dream for them, the legislation that results is likely to achieve something significant.

My friend's son received advice from a teacher that he probably should plan to go to a trade school. However, another teacher encouraged him to pursue academic studies and get the highest degree possible. He eventually received his PhD and is now a research physicist for the navy, where he holds the rank of lieutenant commander. Had he listened only to the first teacher, his future would have dimmed.

The dangers that come with advancing years are not only calcium shortages and stiffer joints, hearing problems and concerns about paying mortgages, but also another terrible affliction: cynicism, and it's contagious. Negative remarks that discourage enthusiastic young people from doing constructive things are exactly what they don't need. With years can come wisdom, and an ability to channel their energy and enthusiasm, but cynical negativism is a disease we don't want to pass on to others. Every contact with a young person is an opportunity to fan the flames of enthusiasm.

Lift your vision.

Lift their vision.

Lift our hopes.

39

ONE OF THE MOST IMPORTANT WORDS IN YOUR LIFE SHOULD BE: VOLUNTEER

YOU'VE ALREADY SEEN THE WORD "VOLUNTEER" USED MANY times on these pages. Leaders are volunteers. People who get things done are volunteers. Some of you reading this can become full-time volunteers in your faith group, at a homeless shelter, with AmeriCorps, or a thousand and one other places where help is needed. If you're a student, there's probably a Volunteer Corps on your campus. Select the area in which you would like to help. Maybe it's the local chapter of the American Cancer Society or a similar group; maybe it's assisting a shelter for abused women and children; perhaps your local library or hospital needs volunteers. International students in your community may need assistance.

If you're tied to your home with children or to long hours at work, remember that your life needs balance. Don't fool yourself into believing that you're doing the right thing for your family if you spend all your free time with them. That's not good for them and not good for you. By example, you should teach them that it's important in life to serve others. If you're not a volunteer already, make as a goal that within the next seven days you'll select a cause or an organization that merits your support. Then surprise yourself and them by volunteering.

If you tend to be shy, it may take an extra effort to volunteer the first time, a little less effort the second time, and the problem will diminish as you volunteer more. If you're a swimmer, you know that feeling of hesitation before you dive into the water that may be cold. Once you're in the water for thirty seconds it feels fine, but the courage it takes to make that first plunge is a barrier.

Your shyness barrier will become smaller and smaller the more you volunteer. Like almost every other good thing, doing it takes a little courage, but it will help you and others.

The Anne Arundel County Public Schools of Maryland started an "I Can Be a Hero" program. They look at the lives of people who have become heroes and how they achieved that status. They discuss what makes an effective leader. While the word "volunteer" appears rarely in the teacher's manual for this program, it is there by implication in everything. Volunteers help themselves and help to build a better society.

Robert Putnam writes: "Community service programs really do strengthen the civic muscle of participants."[29]

If you call a member of the League of Women Voters and mention that you'd like to join their group, you'll receive an enthusiastic welcome. If you call a friend in the Lions, Rotary, Kiwanis, Optimists or any lengthy list of other organizations and tell them you're considering membership, you're likely to become a member quickly. If you're interested in the environment, check out the Sierra Club. There may be a PTA in your area or a chapter of the National Association for the Advancement of Colored People or a branch of the American Association for Retired People—the list goes on and on. We have more voluntary organizations than any nation. It can be an opportunity for you to "spread your wings," to find another avenue of service that broadens your perspective a little.

If you have a disabled child or nephew or niece, perhaps a local group that helps disabled people would be your cup of tea.

A volunteer job often overlooked is giving a caregiver some time off. Sitting with a patient or reading to him or her may be a welcome change for that confined person and particularly helpful for the caregiver.

Ask yourself what cause really interests you. I can almost guarantee you that there's an organization in your area working for that cause.

I forget who had the commercial that applies to volunteering: Try it; you'll like it.

40

LEARN TO RESPECT THE VIEWS
OF OTHERS

AS YOU BECOME MORE INVOLVED IN ISSUES OF ANY KIND, AN important attribute to develop is the ability to "disagree without being disagreeable." This isn't always easy. A reporter once asked me how I was able to maintain good relations with my colleagues in the Senate with whom I frequently strongly disagreed, I said that whenever I get into a debate, I tell myself, "My opponent is just as sincere as I am." Ninety percent of the time this is true. Repeating these words to myself takes the bitter edge off the debate. You can make your points just as effectively but you don't make enemies in the process. It changes the tone of what you say.

After my first wife died of brain cancer, I received generous phone calls from the president and many others, but one call I particularly appreciated came from Senator Jesse Helms, with whom I clashed on the senate floor frequently. My wife would have liked that phone call. It's easy to lose your temper in a debate with someone—but when you lose your temper, you lose. It seems so simple and so obvious to respect the views of others.

Religionists sometimes have a hard time doing this. Religious fanaticism is the cause of most of the small wars and incidents of violence around the world today. Is Osama bin Laden sincere? Yes. Is he wrong? Of course, literally deadly wrong. He never learned to respect the views of others. The zealous haters are a small but dangerous band who exist in every faith group.

During my years in grade school, high school, and college, I don't remember ever encountering "the gay issue." I probably was vaguely aware of it. But when I got into the intelligence branch of the army, I discovered that classified information was not to be given to those with a homosexual orientation for fear of extortion of secrets. Fifty years have passed since that time, and attitudes have changed. But hostility—including physical violence—remains a threat for many who have an openly gay orientation.

Romani, more widely known as Gypsies (a term they don't like), face problems in the United States and even more so in Europe. Their cultural code differs, but few try to learn about their heritage and views. The blunt instruments of hatred and discrimination are easier.

Because someone's views or issues differ from yours and mine doesn't mean we have to accept their approach. But sensible conduct says we should respect the sincerity of those whose beliefs and attitudes differ substantially from ours. We can learn to disagree agreeably.

41

CONVERT A NON-FRIEND
INTO A FRIEND

YOU CAN NEVER HAVE TOO MANY FRIENDS, BUT YOU CAN HAVE too many enemies. It benefits everyone when you can turn a non-friend into a friend. This applies to individuals—and it's also good policy for our nation when dealing with other countries: Student exchanges are better than exchanges of gunfire, visits by tourists are more effective than visits by bombers, understanding one another is better than misunderstanding one another. Individuals, as well as nations, need to do a better job of reaching understandings. This is sometimes difficult to achieve. Usually a combination of creativity, compassion, and common sense will work. In the instances when it doesn't, the blame usually rests a little on both sides.

If there is someone—perhaps a neighbor—with whom relations are not good, plan some small acts of kindness. Perhaps you can turn the grouchy look you've been receiving into a smile. You don't have to be a Christian to recognize the wisdom of the admonition of Jesus: "If your enemy hungers, feed him; if he thirsts, give him something to drink." Try to distinguish between what's important and what's unimportant. So even if your neighbor's tree branches reach over into your yard, it's not the worst thing in the world. Former Secretary of State Henry Kissinger compared campus politics with national politics: "Campus politics are much more bitter because frequently the stakes are so small." There's truth to that. We shouldn't let small things irritate us to the point of bitterness and enmity.

Newt Gingrich, former Speaker of the House, recommended that all politicians read the book *Chimpanzee Politics*. Out of curiosity I got the book. Here's one of the author's observations about chimpanzees:

> After a conflict, the opponents are attracted to each other like magnets. . . . Sometimes the maneuver is fairly obvious. Within a minute of a fight having ended the two former opponents may rush towards each other, kiss and embrace long and fervently and then proceed to groom each other. But sometimes this kind of emotional contact takes place hours after a conflict. . . . Tension and hesitancy remained as long as the opponents had not reconciled their differences.[30]

When asked about the period of the U.S. hostages taken captive in Iran, Ambassador Bruce Laingen, then in charge of our embassy, observed: "Patience is a bitter cup that only the strong can drink."[31]

One participant in the troubled Middle East situation commented, "The real[ly] wise person . . . transforms his enemy into a neighbor and not his neighbor into an enemy."[32]

No one has too many friends. When I served as lieutenant governor of Illinois, two key staff people came to me separately and both said, "The two of us can't get along. You have to fire one of us." I told them that I would make a decision in two weeks. By the end of the two weeks they were getting along famously. One became a United States senator and the other a key leader in major league baseball. To this day they're good friends, working together on various projects of mutual interest.

Converting a non-friend into a friend is always a winning situation for everyone involved.

42

Keep Track of the Extra "Little Things" You Do Each Day to Make Life More Pleasant for Someone

A "LITTLE THING" CAN BE SOMETHING AS SIMPLE AS THANKING a server for the food delivered to your table or a phone call to someone who's ill. You might drop a note of thanks to your mayor for some action he or she has taken; people are quick to complain when they don't like things but rarely offer appreciation. It may be telling your local librarian that you really like the job she or he is doing. You might send a note to someone in the armed forces or serving in the Peace Corps. Mary Muchmore of Carbondale, Illinois, knits and crochets small gifts for people in our armed forces. You might visit a veteran's hospital or a nursing home or someone in your neighborhood who lives alone. Donate clothes you no longer wear to Goodwill or the Salvation Army or take them to a women's center. Contact a relative you seldom see or talk to.

Let this be "Kindness Week" for you. For one week, write down your little acts of kindness. Someone sent my wife a card that said, "Inner beauty reveals itself in outward acts of kindness." I'd heard this before. I don't know who first said it, but it's true. If you try Kindness Week, you may be surprised at how easy it is to do extra "little things" and how appreciated those gestures are.

After one week, you'll probably find yourself in the habit of doing these things more frequently. You'll benefit and so will others.

Make a list of twenty people you know reasonably well. Write down their birthdates, and send him or her a birthday card or pick up the telephone and extend your best wishes on that birthday. It will take only a few minutes of your time, but it is appreciated. My friend Gene Callahan must make at least one hundred calls a year, congratulating people on their birthdays. He has nothing to gain from doing it, other than the satisfaction of pleasing people. And that's a big gain.

Another sensitive person suggests: "If you know people who have had tragedy strike (death of a loved one or a serious injury to a loved one in an accident), mark the date or dates on your calendar and the next year send them a card on the anniversary of the tragedy. This will let them know you are thinking of them and that they are not alone in their sorrow."[33]

When you're driving and someone wants to break into the line of cars or through the line, be a courteous driver. You'll both feel better. When you're at a fast-food drive-through window, surprise the cashier by saying, "Have a great day!" If a new family moves next door, take a box of candy to them. Ask your neighbors to sign a Valentine's Day card for someone from your area away from home in the armed forces or Peace Corps or college. When you see someone you know, greet him or her by name. It's a little recognition that quietly says that person is important to you. If someone ahead of you in line at a restaurant needs three cents to pay a bill, volunteer the three cents. Little courtesies and acts of kindness enrich everyone.

Again, your assignment: For one week, on a sheet of paper, make note of the small acts of friendliness you perform. It will make you more sensitive—and you're likely to continue the habit of small kindnesses.

43

BECOME FAMILIAR WITH THOSE WHO ARE IMPOVERISHED IN YOUR AREA

THE UNITED STATES HAS THE HIGHEST PERCENTAGE OF CHILDREN living in poverty than any of the other major wealthy industrial nations. The readers of this book generally will not be among the poor, and—unless you live in a small community—the difficulties faced by the impoverished are rarely on your mind. Television news programs seldom cover this blemish on our society.

Our culture puts so much emphasis on acquiring things. Because success is usually measured by income, many of those who are really struggling try to hide their poverty. Many don't apply for welfare benefits until they're desperate, and those who do end up among the nation's poor often feel ashamed of their poverty. Many people who use food stamps try to hide the fact and sometimes will wait until no one else is in the grocery line so others don't see them using their food stamps.

Andrew Natsios, administrator of the U.S. Agency for International Development (AID) observes: "All rights are not equal: The right to survive is the most important."[34] That basic right isn't always upheld beyond our borders and even for some within our borders. In the United States, we spend about $2,000 per person annually for health care; in Africa it's only about $10.

Alex Kotlowitz, then a reporter for *The Wall Street Journal,* decided to write a book about problems people face in public housing projects. His book, *There Are No Children Here: The Story of Two Boys Growing Up in the Other America,* brought him into contact with two boys who needed help. He received national awards for his writing, but more important, Alex decided to assist those two boys. When poverty takes on a human face and is more than an abstract statistic, we're much more likely to be moved to action.

Bryen Johnson, a student at Southern Illinois University who lives in the Chicago suburb of Naperville, volunteered to help at a homeless shelter in Aurora, Illinois. What did he learn? "I learned not to judge people. They were smarter and nicer than I expected. The kids were real sweet. It was a great learning experience for me."

Volunteer to work at a homeless shelter or a soup kitchen or some other place where you can learn about and understand the problems that many Americans face. You'll become a more sensitive person—and that can snowball into making a better nation.

44

Expand Your Base of Knowledge and Expand Your Circle of Friends

It's important in life to always keep learning. Be a sponge for information, ask questions about different topics and of people. Find out more about history or global warming or prison systems or your neighbors whose families come from Greece or Poland or Africa. You never know when that little extra you learned will in some way become valuable to you. When an opportunity to make a larger contribution presents itself—and it will, if you recognize it—you'll be better prepared. Everything in life is not calculated.

Grover Cleveland, who later became president of the United States, walked into a restaurant one evening. Three leaders of his political party were meeting, trying to figure out who they could get to run for mayor of Buffalo, New York. Some years earlier, Cleveland had served briefly as a sheriff, and then as an assistant prosecutor. He had a reputation for honesty and ability. His accidental meeting with those leaders led him to become the fiercely independent and courageous mayor of Buffalo, then governor of New York, then president. He had a broad background before he walked into the restaurant, so he was prepared when the opportunity presented itself. I'm not suggesting that you will emerge as president of the United States, but if you do the small things to enrich your background, some special avenue of service will open for you.

When I started my journalism career and then my political career, I had no intention of writing books. After my election to the state legislature, I went to the Illinois State Historical Library and asked for a book about Lincoln's service in the Illinois House of Representatives, the public office he held longer than any other. I was told no such book existed. I wrote to the two names I then identified as Lincoln authors, Carl Sandburg and Allan Nevins, suggesting that they write a book about Lincoln's legislative years. They both wrote back suggesting that I write it. So I launched my first book, which led to others. A little curiosity, combined with a touch of knowledge about Lincoln, has paid off in enriching my life, and I hope has done the same for the small band of readers who buy my books.

"Small things" frequently have unexpected spin-offs. For example, the FBI keeps a record of missing automobiles, but there isn't any record of crimes committed that are motivated by prejudice based on race, religion, sexual orientation, or ethnicity. I introduced a bill to include this area, so we would know more precisely if the poison of prejudice is growing, and if so, where and how much. Two or three years after the bill passed, the head of the FBI called me and said he thought at the time the proposal was of trivial importance. He added that it turned out to be a great thing, but not for the reason I expected. The FBI had sessions with local police units all over the nation on the problems of prejudice in our society. They discovered many conscientious police officers who did not understand the ramifications of intolerance. Requiring the gathering of those statistics turned out to become an important educational tool.

It's the extra things we do to expand our base of knowledge and increase the number of people we know, that will eventually result in improvements.

45

BECOME A BIG BROTHER
OR BIG SISTER

BIG BROTHERS BIG SISTERS IS AN ORGANIZATION THAT encourages responsible citizens to mentor young people who are on the edge of being in trouble. Larry Good of Carbondale, Illinois, for example, learned through his methodist church of someone who faced problems, and he also learned about the Big Brothers Big Sisters organization and volunteered. Big Brothers Big Sisters works with the parents and guardians as well as the courts, local police, or education leaders to help identify children who would be good "Littles" for a Big Brother or Big Sister. These big "brothers and sisters" do an incredible amount of good. In 2002, the organization served more than two hundred thousand youth ages five through eighteen, in five thousand communities across the country, through a network of 470 agencies.

Volunteers go through a background check, including any police records, and then a brief but intensive training program. Larry is a retired teacher, and he says candidly he wishes that he had had the training while he was still teaching; it would have made him a better teacher. He and his wife participate in activities with the young person assigned to him. He likes to give the added touch of taking pictures of their activities together. He gives a set of pictures to the young person he works with. He's now on his second assignment and obviously receives satisfaction from what he's doing. Volunteering as a Big Brother makes his retirement more meaningful—and helps a younger person in ways that can never be calculated, as well as improves our society.

To learn more about the Big Brothers Big Sisters organization, contact them at 230 North 13th Street, Philadelphia, PA 19107, (215) 567-7000, or visit their Web site at www.bbbsa.org.

46

HELP IMPROVE THE HOME
OF A SENIOR CITIZEN
OR DISABLED PERSON

HABITAT FOR HUMANITY, A REMARKABLE ORGANIZATION, builds and repairs homes for people in need. Millard Fuller and his wife, Linda, were in the top one percent income bracket. Everything looked like a great success story for them. But something gnawed at them. They were doing a good job of helping themselves but not at helping others. They had "everything" but they didn't have self-satisfaction. They decided to leave behind all the visible signs of success, move into a small home in rural Americus, Georgia, and start Habitat for Humanity, an organization that has captured the imagination of large numbers of people around the globe, including Jimmy and Rosalyn Carter, the former president and first lady, who continue to devote several days each year to helping Habitat.

There's probably a Habitat chapter near you. The advantage of working with them is that they know from experience the best ways to proceed on projects. But you can also help people in your community with three or four of your friends. Perhaps there's a home in your neighborhood that needs a ramp for a wheelchair or maybe there's a home that needs to be winterized. A Sunday school class in Anna, Illinois, painted a house for residents who couldn't do it themselves or afford to have it done. Many church groups help with "small things" an elderly or disabled person can't do, such as cleaning gutters, tree trimming, or assisting in cleaning. The need for help may be for a mother with three children who can barely buy food and clothing. Many who need help are too proud or too ashamed to ask for it. If you're handy with tools, you can find people with needs not far from where you live.

Or better yet, find out about the local Habitat for Humanity chapter in your area and become a volunteer.

47

Caring Should Result in Sharing

John F. Kavanaugh, SJ, editor of the Roman Catholic publication *America,* believes that in this nation we face five moral challenges and a big one is greed.[35] Learning to share what we have with others is both enlightened and helps us in the long run.

Toward the end of World War II, the GI Bill with its educational benefits for veterans emerged from a House-Senate conference committee by one vote—it was the biggest stride forward for our economy in the last century. The American Legion backed the educational program but the other veterans organizations favored instead a cash bonus of up to $5,000 for returning veterans. The cash bonus had greater popularity; it appealed to our greed, our eagerness to have something now. Fortunately for the nation, the less popular education program prevailed—by one vote. If the cash bonus had prevailed, it would have given a short-term boost to the economy but the benefits couldn't have come anywhere near to the long-term benefits that the GI Bill created.

When we are two or three years old, we learn to share things with others. If one child in a family has many toys and a brother and sister only has a few toys, this would make for family problems. We all can recognize that. But to see the same thing happening in the human family too often escapes us. The United States is the member of the family with many toys, while other members of the human family often lack basic "toys" like food, healthcare, and clean water. This disparity does not help create a healthy and happy human family. We even sometimes sanctify this greed, asserting it makes us a more productive nation. I strongly favor increasing our productivity, but thinly disguised attempts to defend brutal selfishness is as twisted as the "moral" defenses of the economic advantage of having slavery. The lure of personal comfort can lead to twisted thinking. The realistic answer to the world's economic disparity is a greater sharing of the increases in our wealth, and then everyone would benefit. For example, most of us in the United States have rugs in our homes. Most of the world's people don't have rugs, some don't even have flooring, just a dirt floor. The realistic policy answer is not for those who have rugs to give them up, but for those to share more of their economic benefits with others as those benefits increase. How is this done?

More precisely, how can you help do it? Ask yourself two questions: What should the nation be doing? What should I be doing?

On the first question it is both humanitarian and enlightened selfishness to give greater opportunity to those who struggle to get the most basic essentials for life. When the average lifespan in the United States is seventy-seven, but skewed more favorably for whites, and the average lifespan in some nations is forty-two and thirty-seven, it doesn't make sense that the world's wealthiest nation plays a diminishing role in assisting the world's impoverished. Such a world is heading for explosions.

On the question about what you should be doing, you can start by devoting thirty minutes a week to writing legislators and policymakers, urging that we become more responsive to the needy in our nation and in other countries. Add to that a few more minutes each day for reading stories in newspapers and magazines that you may have ignored up to this point about the plight of people who live in circumstances dramatically different from yours.

You can help guide the nation toward better answers. And then do the other things that stretch your mind and your heart and your wallet.

I recently met Joe and Ruth Daniels of Quincy, Illinois, in the St. Louis airport. We had a pleasant conversation—better than pleasant! Inspiring is a more apt description. They used to publish a small newspaper and when they sold it, they had a modest nest egg that they invested wisely. As I talked to them about travel, I learned that they had been on a cruise and met a young Slovak citizen, Robert Hanacek. He was trying to earn enough money to go to college. Joe and Ruth discussed it that evening and the next day told him they would pay his way through college. He attended Westminster College in Missouri, and graduated magna cum laude. The vice president of Westminster College, Patrick Kirby, says "he is such an outstanding student that he has a perfect 4.0 (all A's) grade point average in his coursework at Westminster. He is one of the most outstanding students I have known in my twenty-seven years at Westminster College."[36] He has a fiancée, Andrea Filipcanova, who also wanted to attend college. Joe and Ruth helped her, and Andrea graduated cum laude.

Through the years, Joe and Ruth have assisted ten students who wanted to go to college. Michelle Crider, a young African American, is now a singer at the Metropolitan Opera in New York City. Joe and Ruth have enriched others, and in the process have enriched themselves.

The story of Joe and Ruth Daniels is applicable to each of us and the nation. The Marshall Plan, one of the most generous acts in the history of nations, helped revive the economy of western Europe after World War II, and ultimately, it was of great help to our own economy, even though at the time it was proposed, it stirred a huge controversy in our nation. But we cared, and we shared, and we profited because of it.

The caring and sharing of Joe and Ruth Daniels have not added to their bank account in the way the Marshall Plan paid off for us, but their generosity has in a small but important way helped humanity. And in an account called self-satisfaction, they've become extremely wealthy.

48

BE SENSITIVE ABOUT THE JOKES
YOU TELL AND THE LANGUAGE
YOU USE

JOKES THAT POKE FUN AT SOMEONE'S RELIGION, RACE, SEX, ethnic background, sexual orientation, disability, or physical impairment are not funny. They may get a laugh, but it's a costly laugh. Not many years ago, Polish jokes made the rounds. I even heard the head of a religious denomination tell one. I am sure he meant no harm, but it offended me and certainly offended anyone in the audience whose background is Polish. If you're Danish and you want to tell a joke about Danes, that is better than a non-Dane telling the story, but even telling jokes about people of your background can be easily misconstrued.

Humor can be a lubricant, easing uncomfortable situations. People should take their causes seriously, but not themselves. A light touch, making fun of yourself, is always appreciated. I sometimes quote a Dallas newspaper columnist who wrote about me, "He has a great face for radio." Obviously my television appearance did not impress him! It does me no harm to tell that and it usually gets a chuckle from the audience.

Jokes that are simply crude with references to sexual organs, toilet habits, or simply coarse language will almost always get a response from the audience, mostly out of shock. When a master of ceremonies or someone who precedes me does this, I try to gently disassociate myself from that, usually by referring to the person and saying, "I thought for a short time I was back in the army again." The audience understands and that usually gets a little applause.

When we tell jokes, we are telling something about ourselves. Let your message be that you are a sensitive, understanding person. The same holds true for the language we use.

A distinguished federal judge gave a speech and Nancy Chen, who for several years headed my Chicago office when I served in the Senate, was in the audience. Nancy is Chinese by ethnic background. During the course of the judge's remarks, he used the term "Jap" to refer to someone of Japanese background. Nancy told the judge afterward that many find that term offensive, particularly people of Japanese background. The judge later asked me about it, and I told him he would be wise to stop using that term. Until Nancy Chen spoke to him, no one had ever mentioned this to him. One person who showed a little courage changed his language.

We can tactfully but firmly let people know that jokes they tell or terms they use are inappropriate or offensive. We can start down the right road by being conscious of the jokes we tell and the language we use.

49

LOYALTY SOMETIMES REQUIRES ACTION

THERE ARE MANY WAYS YOU CAN SHOW YOUR LOYALTY. MANY of us serve—or have served—in our armed forces. Helping to create a good library or school system, defending the right of someone to express an unpopular opinion, helping responsible candidates obtain public office are all acts of loyalty. When someone wrongfully criticizes a friend or a family member and you defend him or her, that's also an act of loyalty. Unfortunately, to hear a person defend someone not present from the barbs a loud-mouth uses in attacking him or her, is an act of loyalty that too frequently doesn't happen.

A friend of mine told me of the small town near the farm where he grew up. It had three general stores, but one was not as clean and modern as the other two. Their apples and potatoes didn't receive counter displays, customers had to pick them out of gunny sacks. When my friend suggested to his father that they should shop in one of the more modern stores, his father replied of the older store, "They gave us credit through the depression when we didn't have any money. I'll shop with them until they close." That is loyalty I admire.

Loyalty can have its limits, of course. People should be loyal to their employer, but if he or she requests action that violates basic moral or legal standards, then the employee should notify a superior that he or she cannot follow those orders and will quit the job if necessary. Nazi leaders who killed the Jews said they were simply following orders and being loyal to their nation. There are higher loyalties that all of us should recognize.

Whistleblowers—people who call attention to abuses—are in the finest sense loyal public servants. That requires courage. Whether we're in uniform or out of uniform, loyalty sometimes demands action and sometimes even sacrifice.

50

Don't Fool Yourself

BE HONEST WITH YOURSELF AND OTHERS AND YOU'LL GENERALLY
receive the same treatment in return. Cheating on an exam in
high school or college ultimately means cheating yourself. A person in business who cheats his or her customers may gain temporarily, but most likely not in the long run. When someone
hands you one dollar too much in change, it's easy to remain
silent and pocket that dollar bill, but it's costly to you in the long
run. We try to have a culture of honesty, and generally it works.
It's rare that someone walks out of a restaurant or drives away
from a service station without paying.

Being honest with yourself means recognizing your own flaws
(no one likes to do that), but it also means not letting those flaws
stop you from contributing to society. Being honest with yourself
also means being a person of your word. When you say you'll do
something, do it. If you say you'll be somewhere at a certain time,
be there. And when you make a mistake, be big enough to admit it
and apologize. My guess is that if Richard Nixon had admitted his
mistake in the Watergate scandal and apologized, he wouldn't have
been forced from the presidency. If Bill Clinton had apologized, he
wouldn't have faced an impeachment trial in the Senate. When
Grover Cleveland's opponents charged him with being the father of
a child born out of wedlock, his political advisers told him to deny
it (DNA testing wasn't available back then), but Cleveland admitted it and apologized to the nation. And he won the presidency.

Being honest also requires looking at the status of our culture honestly. I remember speaking at the luncheon of a civic group and I mentioned the problems of poverty. During the question period one member stood up and said, "I don't see any poor people." I'm sure he spoke sincerely and with partial accuracy. Where he lives, where he works, where he attends religious services, and the people he sees at the luncheon meetings are not poor. But we shouldn't fool ourselves into believing that the narrow focus of our lives accurately reflects what's happening in society and the world.

In Illinois, for example, one of the wealthiest states with 12.5 million people, are 1,668,000 non-elderly citizens without health insurance. Slightly more than 10 percent of its population lives at or below the federal poverty line. Chicago's poor would constitute the twelfth largest city in the United States. More than one in three adults living in poverty in Illinois do not have a high school diploma.[37] These statistics reflect a part of Illinois—and whatever state you live in—that most people do not really see and understand.

We all can benefit from a culture in which we are honest with each other and ourselves.

51

Don't Agonize over Decisions Already Made

MAKE A DECISION CAREFULLY, BUT ONCE YOU MAKE IT, MOVE ON to other things. Agonizing over decisions already made can give you ulcers and make you less effective. I can hear you say, "That's more easily said than done." It's true that different personalities will respond in dissimilar ways. However, there is a method of reducing whatever tensions you may feel about a decision that is now history: Start working on something else right away. The people who contribute immensely are not the men and women who have never made a mistake in judgment, but rather the people who don't let that decision, which may be wrong or right or unpopular, become a barrier to their future service.

Mihaly Csikszentmihalyi, a psychologist who studied the field of enjoyment, watched and photographed artists while they painted. He wrote: "One of the things that struck me was the almost trance-like state they entered when the work was going well." Then when the artists finished the canvas they "almost immediately lost interest. . . . Typically they turned the finished canvas around and stacked it against a wall. . . . They could hardly wait to start a new one."[38] It's important to look to the future rather than agonize over the past.

Every author will reach a point when he or she questions, "I wonder if anyone will read this book. Will it sell?" But those thoughts pass quickly, and months before this manuscript is available in book form, I'm sure I'll sign a contract to write another book, rather than ruminate over this completed manuscript.

One of my abler colleagues in the U.S. Senate (from another state) sometimes worried for weeks after casting a controversial vote. For him to be concerned before the vote was wise. Reliving and regurgitating that vote again and again after the decision had been made prevented him from being as effective a senator as he could have been.

Whatever field of work you're in, or if you're retired, you'll still have to make difficult decisions from time to time. Make them and then move on to the next constructive action you can take. That's good for society—and helps prevent you from getting ulcers!

52

Don't Let Age Be a Barrier to Doing Good Things, to Dreaming

IN THIS BOOK YOU HAVE READ ABOUT A NINE-YEAR-OLD providing leadership and many who are much, much older giving us a better direction. Age, whether young or old, should never stop you from going for your dreams, from making something happen. In these days when Christian-Jewish-Muslim relationships have become so important and so entangled, Bernard Lewis is often quoted. He is a retired faculty member from Princeton, and few people know or would guess that he is eighty-six years old.

A few miles from me in agricultural southern Illinois, Wayman Presley, who retired at sixty-five as a rural mail carrier, decided to start a travel business in Makanda, Illinois, population 402. At one point before his death, his was the fourth largest travel agency in the United States. Age didn't slow down Wayman. It shouldn't stop you.

I mentioned Carol Channing in an earlier chapter. She is eighty-three years old. If she has slowed her pace, it isn't apparent.

Howard Metzenbaum, from Ohio, served in the Senate. He prevented more bad legislation than any member of that body. He and his staff looked through proposals with a legislative microscope, and the threat of a Metzenbaum amendment usually brought improved language to a bill. While his reputation resulted in the media identifying him as a liberal, and in many ways that applied to him, he stopped more nonsense from becoming law than any member. That should have resulted in honors from a conservative organization.

Howard has retired from the Senate. But at eighty-six years old, he is the chair of the board of the Consumer Federation of America, he is on the board of Public Citizen and half a dozen other groups, and in his spare time, he plays tennis and attends a variety of public functions. He could be in Florida, relaxing on the beach, which he does sometimes. But Howard, and his equally energetic wife, Shirley, are using their later years to enrich others.

One of the most courageous men I've known is also from Ohio, former Senator John Glenn. We retired from the Senate the same year. He was the first American sent into space, and if you can imagine the tiny capsule that he squeezed into for the first U.S. space flight, it took an incredible amount of courage to be that pioneer. It also required courage for his wife, Annie, who showed a different display of courage in overcoming a serious stuttering problem as the wife of a public official. At the age of seventy-five John Glenn volunteered to go into space again, to test, among other things, the impact of space flight on the body and mind of someone his age. He could have spent his life playing golf or doing other pleasant activities. Instead, at the age of seventy-five, he continues to inspire all of us.

Ruth Elizabeth Kenney was the oldest of six children in a farm family in Perry County, Illinois. At the age of sixty, while she was visiting her diabetic husband Walter in the hospital in Carbondale, Illinois, she noticed that nurses were holding babies, soothing them, and giving them love and attention. She asked if they needed help, since she had done that many times as the oldest child in her large farm family and as the mother of four. Before she could change her mind, she had a job. She held that position for nineteen years, getting to know the habits of babies well enough to know if there were problems that needed medical attention. She's credited with saving at least one baby's life—and probably a lot more. During those nineteen years she cradled and comforted approximately fifteen thousand babies. They named the nursery in the hospital after her. But the big tribute is that this woman, who accidentally started this work at the age of sixty, died thirty years ago—and people still talk about her and remember her with gratitude.

The most widely known surgeon general of the United States in my lifetime was Dr. C. Everett Koop, an appointee of Ronald Reagan. He wrote: "I have learned at eighty-five you can still do two full-time jobs, and as a matter of fact, I think the reason I can say this at eighty-five is that I have never stopped working, and working hard, and trying to make a difference."[39]

One friend wrote to me: "We should keep serving, thinking, reading, and energizing after sixty-five. I am now eighty-five and I am not languishing on the shelf. But I am not as quick mentally or as supple physically as I used to be. My tempo has to be slower. My involvements have to be fewer and carefully edited." As long as he keeps "serving, thinking, reading, and energizing" I will not quarrel with him.

And whether you're a fan of General Douglas MacArthur, you should be able to appreciate his comment: "People grow old only by deserting their ideals. Years may wrinkle the skin, but to give up interest wrinkles the soul."[40]

Richard and Lucille Baughman of Springfield, Illinois, are both in their eighties and recently celebrated their sixty-sixth wedding anniversary. They have been hospital volunteers for about twenty years. They have the satisfaction of helping others. Their grandson told me, "They probably have lived longer because they feel needed and appreciated and are part of something constructive. They're not just sitting at home getting older."

Studs Terkel, the prize-winning author, is always working on another book—and probably has six more in the back of his head. He is ninety-one years old. The other day he tried to enlist me in the cause of one of the candidates for president of the United States. All of us who know him or have heard him speak or read his books know that he is a national treasure who fortunately didn't let age prevent him from his humanitarian endeavors.

If you are older than sixty-five, don't stop contributing.

If you are younger than sixty-five, remember that many who have topped that age find themselves with little to do. Get a senior citizen involved in a project of yours. It will be good for that person and good for your cause.

ENDNOTES

1. *Chicago,* lyrics by Fred Ebb.
2. Robert Putnam, *Bowling Alone* (New York: Simon and Schuster, 2000), 224.
3. "Writing in Schools Is Found Both Dismal and Neglected," by Tamar Lewin, *New York Times,* 26 April 2003.
4. "Why We Tuned Out," by Karen Springne, *Newsweek,* 11 November 2002.
5. "Longitudinal Relations between Children's Exposure to TV Violence and Their Aggressive and Violent Behavior in Young Adulthood: 1977–1992," by Russell Huesmann, Jessica Moise-Titus, Cheryl-Lynn Podalski, and Leonard Eron, *Developmental Psychology,* 2003, Vol. 39, No. 2.
6. Testimony before the Senate Subcommittee on Science, Technology, and Space, 10 April 2003.
7. "With Mark Twain You Can Get Away with Murder," Andrew Card interview with Hal Holbrook, *American Heritage,* August/September 2003.
8. Putnam, 67.
9. The Civic Mission of Schools, no author indicated (New York: Carnegie Corporation, 2003) 11, quoting from *Voice and Equality: Civic Voluntarism in American Politics,* Sidney Verba, et al (Cambridge: Harvard University Press, 1995).
10. Interview with Kathleen Kastlihan, "When Religion Becomes Evil," *The Lutheran,* July 2003.
11. Charles Kimball, *When Religion Becomes Evil* (New York: Harper, 2002), 129.

12. Besides these series, which are readily available in major bookstores or on-line, check your local library or the Internet for additional books. Many fine books on understanding the Islamic faith have been written recently.

13. Millard Fuller, *Building Materials for Life* (Macon, Ga.: Smyth and Helwys, 2002), 92.

14. Arthur Simon, *How Much Is Enough?* (Grand Rapids, Mich.: Baker Books, 2003), 130.

15. Quoted in "One Student at a Time" by Anne Constable, *The New Mexican* (Santa Fe), 28 November 2002.

16. Quoted in "The Seven Sins of American Foreign Policy" by Loch K. Johnston, University of Georgia, and Kiki Caruson, University of South Florida, *PS* (Political Science), January 2003.

17. Quoted on *The Tim Russert Show,* CNBC, 17 May 2003.

18. Quoted in "The Selling of America, Bush Style," by Victoria DeGrazia, *The New York Times,* 25 August 2002.

19. *Every Day Heroes,* no author indicated (Langley, Wash.: Giraffe Project, 1997), 59, 86-89.

20. "Catch and Release," by Margaret Talbot, *Atlantic Monthly,* January/February 2003.

21. Bulletin of Citizens United for Rehabilitation of Errants (Katonah, N.Y.), 16 July 2003.

22. Quoted in "A Complicated Life," by Jesse Green, *New York Times Magazine,* 6 July 2003.

23. "The Mind of George W. Bush," by Richard Brookhiser, *Atlantic Monthly,* April 2003. The speechwriter quoted is David Frum.

24. "Won't You Help Feed Them?" by David Relin, *Parade,* 27 April 2003.

25. Quoted in "Chaos to Progress: One School's Turbulent Tale," by Elizabeth Duffrin, *Catalyst Chicago,* February 2000.

26. "We Don't Have to Be Saints," by Paul Loeb, *Oregon Quarterly*, Summer 2003.

27. Putnam, 402.

28. Millard Fuller, *More Than Houses* (Nashville: Word Publishing, 2000), xii.

29. Putnam, 405.

30. Frans de Waal, *Chimpanzee Politics* (Baltimore, Md.: Johns Hopkins University Press, 1989), 40-41.

31. Statement in address at Southern Illinois University, 28 April 2003.

32. "Winning the Enemy," by Mtri Raheb, *The Lutheran,* July 2002.

33. Terry Gump, note to Paul Simon, 10 July 2003.

34. Quoted in "Advancing Human Rights and Peace in a Complex World," Special Report of U.S. Institute of Peace (Washington, D. C.) 22 April 2002.

35. "Five Moral Crises," by John F. Kavanaugh, *America,* 6-13 January 2003.

36. Reference letter, Patrick T. Kirby, 5 March 2003.

37. 2003 Report on Illinois Poverty, compiled by Rob Paral (Chicago: Heartland Alliance, 2003).

38. Quoted from *Beyond Boredom and Anxiety,* by Mihaly Csikszentmihalyi, in *Enough: Staying Human in an Engineered Age,* by Bill McKibben (New York: Times Books, 2003), 50-51.

39. Quoted in *The Older the Fiddle, the Better the Tune,* edited by Willard Scott (New York: Hyperion, 2003), 155-156.

40. Ibid, 171.

ABOUT THE AUTHOR

Paul Simon (1928-2003) was a pro-
fessor at Southern Illinois University,
where he taught classes in political science, history, and journalism. He joined
SIU's faculty in 1997—just weeks after
retiring from the U.S. Senate. Simon
made his home in Makanda, Illinois
(population 402). Simon was founder
and director of the Public Policy
Institute at the Carbondale campus. The

Institute opened its doors in 1997 and promises to "find new ways
of solving some very old problems," said Simon.

Simon was born November 29, 1928, in Eugene, Oregon.
He attended the University of Oregon and Dana College in Blair,
Nebraska. At the age of nineteen, Simon became the nation's
youngest editor-publisher when he accepted a local Lion's Club
challenge to save the *Troy Tribune* in Troy, Illinois, near St. Louis.
He built a chain of thirteen newspapers in southern and central
Illinois, which he sold in 1966 to devote full-time to public ser-
vice and writing.

In 1960, Paul Simon married Jeanne Hurley of Wilmette,
whom he met while both served in the Illinois House. Jeanne
Simon died in February 2000. They had two children and four
grandchildren. In May 2001, he married Patricia Derge, the
widow of a former SIUC president, David Derge.

Simon was elected to the U.S. House of Representatives in
1974 and served Illinois' 22nd and 24th Congressional Districts
for ten years. During his service in the House, Simon played a

leading role in drafting and enacting major legislation in a wide range of issue areas including education, disability policy, and foreign affairs. In 1984, Simon upset three-term incumbent Charles Percy to win election to the U.S. Senate. In 1987-88, he sought the Democratic nomination for president. He won re-election to the U.S. Senate in 1990 by defeating Congresswoman Lynn Martin with 65 percent of the vote.

During his years as a public official, Paul Simon was known for exceptional constituent service. His office handled more cases each year than almost any other senate office. He also was the Senate's pacesetter in convening town meetings. As a senator, Simon held more than six hundred town meetings throughout the state, more than any U.S. senator from Illinois in the state's history. For forty consecutive years—longer than any other federal officeholder—Simon released an annual detailed financial disclosure report for himself and his wife.

Simon held more than fifty-five honorary degrees and had written twenty-two books (four with co-authors). For more about Paul Simon, go to http://www.siu.edu/~ppi.